Rein
Selected Writi

Reiner Schürmann

Neo-Aristotelianism and the Medieval Renaissance:
On Aquinas, Ockham, and Eckhart

Lecture Notes for Courses at
the New School for Social Research

Spring 1978/Spring 1991

Edited by
Ian Alexander Moore

DIAPHANES

Reiner Schürmann
Selected Writings and Lecture Notes

Edited by Francesco Guercio, Michael Heitz,
Malte Fabian Rauch, and Nicolas Schneider

1st edition
ISBN 978-3-0358-0148-4
© DIAPHANES, Zurich 2020
All rights reserved.

Layout: 2edit, Zurich
Printed in Germany

www.diaphanes.com

Table of Contents

Syllabus

Aristotle was rediscovered in the West in the thirteenth century. Three aspects will be studied: 1) The main figure of medieval Aristotelianism was Thomas Aquinas. His ontology will be exposed through the transformation undergone in his philosophy by such Aristotelian notions as analogy, substance, categories, causality, teleology. Some consequences of these transformations for the understanding of man will be shown. 2) Aristotelianism entails a greater emphasis on sense experience than neo-Platonism. In William of Ockham sense experience became the sole cause of knowledge, hence the 'nominalist' rejection of universals in his doctrine. 3) Late medieval speculative mysticism (Meister Eckhart and Nicholas of Cusa) forced Aristotelian intuitions into yet another direction: e.g. the abolition of the distinction between created and uncreated.

Plan of Lectures[1]

I. The several senses of Being in Thomas Aquinas:
   a) Being as "being real."
   b) Being as "being a thing."
   c) "Analogy of Being."

II. Aquinas' Philosophy of Knowledge:
   a) The pre-modern relationship of "subject" and "object."
   b) Vegetative, sensitive, and intellectual life and the ideas of connaturality.
   c) Knowledge by connaturality and the "active intellect."

III. William of Ockham's conceptualism:
   a) The critique of connaturality and of the active intellect.
   b) The universal "is only in the soul and hence not in the thing."
   c) Sign and conventionality.

IV. Meister Eckhart's and Cusanus' speculative mysticism:
   a) A practical imperative as the condition for thinking.
   b) The "coincidence of opposites."

Literature

Texts used

— Pegis, Anton C., ed. *Introduction to St. Thomas Aquinas*. New York: Modern Library, 1948.
— William of Ockham. *Philosophical Writings: A Selection*. Translated by Philotheus Boehner. Indianapolis: Bobbs-Merrill, 1964.
— Blakney, Raymond Bernard, ed. *Meister Eckhart*. New York: Harper & Row, 1941.
— Master Eckhart. *Parisian Questions and Prologues*. Translated by Armand A. Maurer. Toronto: Pontifical Institute of Medieval Studies, 1974.
— Nicholas of Cusa. *Unity and Reform: Selected Writings*. Translated by John Patrick Dolan. Notre Dame, IN: University of Notre Dame Press, 1962.

Recommended secondary literature

— Brentano, Franz. *On the Several Senses of Being in Aristotle*. Translated by Rolf George. Berkeley: University of California Press, 1975.
— Owens, Joseph. *An Interpretation of Existence*. Milwaukee: Bruce, 1968.
— Chenu, Marie Dominique. *Towards Understanding St. Thomas*. Translated by Albert M. Landry and Dominic Hughes. Chicago: Regnery, 1964.
— Gilson, Étienne. *The Christian Philosophy of St. Thomas Aquinas*. Translated by L. K. Shook. New York: Random House, 1956.
— Henle, R. J. *Saint Thomas and Platonism: A Study of the Plato and Platonici Texts in the Writings of Saint Thomas*. The Hague: M. Nijhoff, 1956.
— Klubertanz, G. P. *St. Thomas on Analogy: A Textual Analysis and Systematic Synthesis*. Chicago: Loyola University Press, 1960.
— Rahner, Karl. *Spirit in the World*. Translated by William Dych. Montreal: Palm, 1968.
— Boehner, Philotheus. *Collected Articles on Ockham*. 2nd ed. Edited by Eligius Maria Buytaert. St. Bonaventure, NY: The Franciscan Institute, 1992.
— Royce, Jossiah. "Meister Eckhart." In *Studies of Good and Evil: A Series of Essays upon Problems of Philosophy and of Life*. Hamden, CT: Archon Books, 1964.
— Cassirer, Ernst. *The Individual and the Cosmos in Renaissance Philosophy*. Translated by Maria Domandi. Oxford: Basil Blackwell, 1963.

Introduction

Aristotle and the Medieval Renaissance

Let me begin by 'situating' the High Middle Ages and its Aristotelianism by some brief remarks on the cultural history.

a. Medieval Renaissance. Under the Carolingian Frankish dynasty Europe had known a first revival in the ninth century, called the Carolingian Renaissance. Its innovative thinker was John Scotus Eriugena. What is properly called The Renaissance, i.e., the revival in the fifteenth and sixteenth centuries, is a secular, 'humanist' return to Antiquity, whereas the Carolingian was much more spiritual. In between these two renaissances—which, in a sense, open and close the Middle Ages—there occurs what should properly be called the Medieval Renaissance. This is neither primarily spiritual nor, certainly, secular in nature. It is indistinguishably intertwined with the discovery, or re-discovery, of Aristotle.

The Carolingian Renaissance is feudal, imperial: Charlemagne dreamt of reviving the Roman Empire. It is also, on an extremely feeble textual basis, neo-Platonist: Scotus Eriugena construes an idealist philosophy from extremely fragmentary information about the tradition. Finally, it is rationalist, and in this sense retrieves the greatest elements of the late Roman Empire, namely the learning in grammar and the 'trivium' altogether. This juncture of grammar as paradigmatic science and idealist neo-Platonism is such a natural alliance that one could even define neo-Platonism as the method of hypostatizing grammatical elements. Culturally, this confluence of Roman grammar and Platonic inwardness—perhaps joined by feudal and imperial representations of hierarchy—contributes to an understanding of the first renaissance.

The second renaissance, in the thirteenth century, rests on two bases: the revival of Roman law at the University of Bologna in the twelfth century, and the revival of Aristotelian science of nature at the University of Paris in the thirteenth century. One has to see the reversal with regard to the previous renaissance: Roman law challenged, in fact, theocratic aspirations and pretense. The justification

13

of government ceased to be based, progressively, on biblical symbolism and became more empirical. The same turn of the mind attracts physicians and scientists towards Aristotle.[2] Historically, theocratic aspirations had lost, once and for all, with the victory of the French king Philippe II over the Holy Roman Emperor Otto IV (at Bouvines, 1214). The second renaissance coincides thus with a decline of the feudal hierarchy and particularly with the rise of the medieval communes and towns. Neo-Platonic Augustinianism belongs to the context of landed aristocracy, of self-sufficient monasteries, of the unchallenged rule of an authority. Aristotelianism belongs to the cities. There the universities, in the Medieval Renaissance, offer the climate for sections of knowledge—primarily in medicine, law, science of nature—to become autonomous with regard to religion. Such an autonomy of branches of knowledge was unthinkable in the context of the first renaissance. The monastic schools are replaced by universities—to understand this shift is to understand the background for the immense attraction towards Aristotle in the thirteenth century. Feudal conservatism had retreated behind the rise of townspeople with their competition, their availability for new ways of academic careers, and with, actually, new religious orders. The teaching of the older orders remained mainly Augustinian and neo-Platonic; it is the new orders that discover in Aristotle a chance for secular learning. The denial of knowledge established independently from religion is only the ideology of feudal conservatism.

One word, in this context, about the third renaissance: it develops further the drive towards scientific and artistic autonomy from faith. Mainly in literature and visual arts, the revival of Greek ideals contests a monolithic Christianity.

The second renaissance is actually unthinkable without the background of Paris and its university. Paris is called the 'new Athens': there is no clearer way of indicating the renaissance. Here is one text, from the end of the thirteenth century, about this role of Paris in the learning of the High Middle Ages: "The blessed Dionysius the Areopagite came to Paris in order to make this city into the mother of studies, in the manner of Athens. And quite as Athens, the city of Paris is divided into three parts: the first is that of the merchants, craftsmen and the populace, it is called the great city; the second is that of the aristocrats where the king's court is located as well as the cathedral, it is called 'la cité'; the third is that of the students and the colleges, it is called the University. Learning was first transmitted from Greece to Rome, and then, at the time of Charlemagne, from Rome to Paris... "[3] The 'nationes' made up the international crowd of what is still called the Latin Quarter. The small entity of the university actually must be considered as a renaissance of the cosmopolitan character of the Roman Empire.

b. Neo-Aristotelianism. Whereas neo-Platonism is a new intellectual breed, a new Platonism, neo-Aristotelianism, since it stood for a retrieval of autonomous learning, is Aristotelianism little-transformed—at least in the doctrines that first made Aristotle so attractive to a mind dissatisfied with the totalitarian rule of faith over knowledge: logic and the science of nature. In neo-Platonism, the 'neo' indicates a new brand of Platonism; in neo-Aristotelianism, it simply indicates a rebirth of Aristotelianism.

But to speak of rebirth implies imitation, obedience to ancient models. The second renaissance is not as free and creative as the great Renaissance; the chief literary genus in the thirteenth century remains the 'commentary,' either of the Bible or of Aristotle, simply called, ever since approximately 1250, 'the Philosopher.' This 'deferential exposition' is considered a scandal in the Quattrocento. It also carries within it the germ of dogmatism, scholasticism precisely. We are thus faced with the paradox that the return to Aristotle was animated by the passion for purer air, more rigorous methods, greater autonomy of reason—but that the so-called 'School,' over the century, came to stand more and more for the contrary of precisely its early ideals. In the sixteenth century, Cajetan defends its positions against Luther quite as in the thirteenth century the church condemned Thomas Aquinas' Aristotelianism as dangerous (1277). The medieval rational genius has to rely on a datum, a text, an *auctoritas* [authority], be that religious or not. But this reliance, as will be seen, by no means precludes an entirely new thinking: it is the deed of the medieval Aristotelians to expand some of Aristotle's intuitions into what is, properly, another context.

To Boethius only the *Categories* and *On Interpretation* were known; he was the translator of these texts, and his translations remained the sole source until the early twelfth century.[4] Then, within a century and a half the entire Aristotelian corpus became available in Latin, mainly by way of the Arabs.

Albert the Great appreciated mainly the Aristotelian treatises on animals. "In matters of faith and morals, one has to believe Augustine rather than the philosophers; in questions of medicine, I trust Galen and Hippocrates; and concerning the nature of things it is of Aristotle that I seek advice."[5] Until 1250, the rest of Aristotle is considered dangerous. This is important! Together with the emphasis on logic, the Aristotelian legacy disrupts the unity of religion and philosophy; with such innocent considerations as forms of reasoning and the parts of animals, philosophy breaks away from its subservient position with regard to religion—at least it begins to break away. The introduction of Aristotelianism thus implies a new status given to philosophy, a negation of the realism of universals; an intelligence turned towards the earth, becoming 'naturalist.' The physical world now becomes intelligible in itself: such is the immediate effect of the rediscovery of Aristotle. In one word, philosophy emancipates itself from religion (be that Christian, as in Augustine et al., or non-Christian, as in Plotinus and Proclus).

The translations resulted from the contact, not only with the Arabs, but also with the Greeks in Constantinople. In that respect it remains hardly understandable how Aristotle could be known so thoroughly whereas of Plato hardly any text was known at all. So: there is a direct reception of Aristotle (the great names are: Bartholomew of Messina, Robert Grosseteste, William of Moerbecke) and an indirect one: from Greek into Syriac into Arabic, perhaps into ancient Spanish, into Latin![6]

c. *Albert the Great.* Albert is the one who introduces the Aristotelian corpus into philosophy; he is called the 'doctor universalis' because of his immense culture and writing, and his disciple Ulrich of Strasburg calls him 'Nostri temporis stupor et miraculum' [Wonder and marvel of our times].[7] What does Albert's Aristotelianism look like? Three themes:

1) Active intellect. Albert identifies the Christian Creator God with the Aristotelian active intellect. But something totally heretical, for an Aristotelian, is introduced when he says: the 'intellectus

universaliter agens' [universally active intellect] causes the first created intelligence to exist which, in turn, creates all things visible. From this first created intelligence, he says, all things 'emanate' in degrees, through the world soul, down to material beings. The mixture of traditions is evident: the fragment from Proclus titled the *Liber de Causis* is as much of an influence here as Aristotle. Also, Albert states explicitly: "You have to know that man will never become perfect in philosophizing unless by the science of the two philosophies, that of Aristotle and that of Plato."[8] The concept of active intellect is introduced by Albert to break up a monist concept of being: the being of the first intelligence is not God's—we shall see in detail (in Thomas Aquinas) how the Aristotelian Metaphysics is used to counter a univocal notion of being as it is operative, for instance, in Eriugena, and differently in [Duns] Scotus. It is the homogeneous world-representation of the neo-Platonists that Albert refuses when he says: "Some held that all things are one and that the diffusion of the first being in all of them is their being," but that is not so ("Quidam dixerunt, omnia esse unum et quod diffusio primi in omnibus est esse eorum").[9] Indeed, Albert would gather from Aristotle's notion of the 'nous poiētikos' [active intellect], however sparse the notation in *De Anima* III, 5 may be, that it is unmixed, unaffected, creative, autonomous. When the 'nous poiētikos' is identified with the unmoved mover, as is the case in Albert's Aristotelianism, the concept of motion is used to disrupt a monistic metaphysics as inherited from Eriugena: the reasoning about the unmoved mover as it is developed in *Physics* VII, 1; VIII, 5 & 6 and in *Metaphysics* XII, 6, begins with the observation that all that is moved is moved by another. This starting point is the premise for all neo-Aristotelian proofs of the existence of God (vs. ontological arguments): whatever is not moved by itself must be moved by another, and: *non est recedere in infinitum* [there is no infinite regress]. The idea of 'other' introduces difference into an ontology of identity. The quote from Albert shows that clearly. Thus, although the reasoning about creation is carried out in the schemes of emanation by Albert, the concept of otherness as it is developed from the active intellect and the unmoved mover puts an end to emanationist monism. Such monism, as we shall see, is rejected by all neo-Aristotelians in their doctrine of the analogy of being.

2) The universals. On this point, Peter Abelard is sometimes called the first medieval Aristotelian. He mediates between an extreme nominalism (Roscelin and, later, Ockham) that holds that only individuals exist and that a universal is only a 'flatus vocis,' a word we breathe, and an extreme realism (much more prominent until the twelfth century, and then held by William of Champeaux) which claims that common nature is real, that it is wholly present in each individual, which, therefore, differ from one another only by accidents, but not substantially. The Aristotelians, ever since Abelard and Albert, will say, on the contrary: 'substantiae simpliciter diversae' [substances are simply different]. Both Abelard and Albert distinguish, then, between a universal 'ante rem' [before the thing], 'in re' [in the thing], and 'post rem' [after the thing]. 'Ante rem': the specific essence or nature of a thing is independent of its realization in one given thing—but that does not mean that it exists by itself, only that an empirical datum in its individuality is logically 'after' the universal essence. 'In re': the universal is the form of the thing, and cannot be encountered elsewhere than in the thing. 'Post rem': the universal is abstracted from the thing and thus 'later' enters our mind. In Abelard and Albert, then, the habit of philosophizing from grammar as if the logical and the real order were the same, receives its death blow. For the neo-Aristotelians the logical and the real orders are parallel, but not identical. The universal thus names things that really exist; the universal is not just mere sound. Abelard and Albert differ, however, when it comes to ascribing a locus to the universal 'in re': for Abelard, universals are not located in the noun—a man—but in the verb or predicate: being a man. Properly speaking, then, for Abelard the 'in re' is displaced towards the proposition about the thing. Nevertheless, the neo-Aristotelian 'middle of the road' solution which characterizes Albert and Aquinas is inaugurated with Abelard.

3) The substance of the soul. At first sight, a Christian philosophy that remains within the realm of the subject-matters assigned to it by faith seems to be bound to a Platonizing concept of soul: if the soul is immortal, it cannot simply be understood in the Aristotelian fashion as the form of the human body. But the doctrine of the soul and its autonomy are more Platonic in Aristotle himself—the active intellect, being of divine origin, "enters from without" into

man (*De Gen. Anim.* B 3; 736 b 27); the spiritual soul thus seems to be essentially immaterial, separate, substantial. This difficulty is expressed in the *De Anima*: "the soul by which we live, perceive, and think" (414 a 12) "alone is capable of existing in isolation from all other psychic powers ... differing as what is eternal from what is perishable" (413 b 27). Albert pursues this Aristotelian doctrine of the substantiality of the soul in the vocabulary inherited from Boethius: one cannot say that the soul is utterly simple, because then it would be uncreated and God. Nor can one say that it is composed of matter and form, for then it would not be itself the form of the human being. It must therefore be composed otherwise, and Boethius and Albert say: of *quo est* and *quod est*, i.e., of essence and existence. If such a composition can be predicated of the soul, it is something concrete and an individual substance. But Albert goes, of course, further than Aristotle in affirming the substantiality of the soul when Albert says: it is not the entelechy of the body. If it were, its substantiality would be done with. He calls the soul, then, the helmsman of the body: a Platonic metaphor which recurs, however, in Aristotle's *Physics*, Book VIII.

From these three elements, on which Albert's Aristotelianism hinges, I take the plan of this course: we shall first deal with the problem of identity and difference in medieval Aristotelian ontology, more precisely: "The Several Senses of Being in Thomas Aquinas"; we shall then consider the problems of the soul in connection with "Aquinas' Philosophy of Knowledge"; after that we shall address the question of universals for their own sake, although out of one author alone: "William of Ockham's Conceptualism." After these three main points of discussion I shall append a section on "Meister Eckhart's and Cusanus' Speculative Mysticism"[10] with the following goal: one reads time and again that late medieval speculative mysticism is a return of neo-Platonic themes, pushed to their extreme consequences. That is only partially true. I shall show that, on the contrary, both Eckhart and Cusanus rely on basically Aristotelian notions in their speculative mysticism.

d. The concept of medieval philosophy. The unity of medieval philosophy, or its very possibility and limit, can be approached (and I have done it in other courses[11]) from many angles. Here I should like to present it in reference to the Carolingian Renaissance. Indeed, the Carolingian and the High Medieval Renaissance stand in continuity so that, independently from the debate between Platonic and Aristotelian traditions, one can see a return to the ninth century in the very discovery of Aristotle. This appears again from the point of view of cultural history, and in three points:

[1)] The cultural rootedness of medieval philosophy.[12] The Carolingian Renaissance was the intellectual effort to integrate, on the explicit injunction of the emperor, 'higher learning' into the public life of the empire. It is significant here that Charles II, The Bold, charged Eriugena with the translation of the works of Dionysius the Areopagite[13] and with instituting the imperial school at his court. Higher learning, in the Carolingian Renaissance, is a way to spread quasi-theocratic feudalism into everyday life. After the irruption of Aristotle, the modalities of such cultural rootedness change: the university is now the mediator between higher learning and the spiritual needs of society. Nevertheless, philosophy and theology are servants to the medieval order of life—rather than calling philosophy the servant of theology. In the thirteenth century, these cultural needs are much more sophisticated than in the ninth, but the fact that Aquinas' theses were condemned is but one eloquent indication of the university's mission to shape a culture.

[2)] The religious horizon of medieval philosophy. The assignment given by Charles II to Scotus Eriugena entailed a reorganization of the entire knowledge available in the ninth century in terms of biblical faith. Something similar is still at work in the High Middle Ages: faith establishes the horizon within which 'natural light' can proceed according to its own rules. It is insufficient to speak of the 'ancilla' [handmaiden] character of philosophy: rather, theology decides which questions enter at all into the horizon of reason, and which are not relevant, not present, for that period. Religion establishes the field within which secular reason may operate.

[3)] The renaissance of liberal arts. The term 'philosophia' designates, both in the ninth and the thirteenth centuries, the seven liberal arts together. Aquinas calls them the 'philosophicae disciplinae.' They are, in their subject matter and method, exclusively taken from the natural functioning of reason—but in either renaissance determined by the achievements of antiquity. At the same time, this double renaissance exhibits, in each field, an unsatisfactory or incomplete status of answers given by the 'lumen naturale' [natural light]: the seven liberal arts point towards faith as their necessary complement. In Eriugena's teaching of predestination, secular reason is able to establish human freedom; but the concept of freedom so obtained is then tied to redemption in Christ. In modern terms: medieval anthropology is deficient Christology. This does not restrict the autonomy of reason, but it assigns to human reason its site of competence. There are questions that can be answered by reason alone; there are other ones that require revelation. These latter ones shed the ultimate light on the first ones.

I.

The Several Senses of Being in
Thomas Aquinas

Philosophy has never been more preoccupied—Aristotle and Heidegger excepted—with being than in the High Middle Ages. The reason for this lies partly in the religious tradition that assigns, as I said, to philosophy its field: in the Book of Exodus God is said to have said—that is how the Medievals translate an enigmatic statement, at least—of himself: "Ego sum qui sum" [I am who I am]. But to this problematic of being, my remarks on the status of reason in the Middle Ages apply most evidently: the problematic of ontology is drafted by a non-philosophical tradition and insight; but the way this problematic is carried out, relying as it does on Aristotle, turns against such dependence. The main point that I want to make in these lectures about Aquinas is: his notion of being carries into the heart of metaphysics the autonomy of reason discovered in logic and the natural sciences. To state it in his language: the being we primarily talk of when we say 'to be' is the sensible substance—in Aristotle's language, the sub-lunar world as it can be experienced. Such an empirical being is called 'ens.'

In *Metaph.* IV, 2; 1003 b 6 Aristotle wrote:

> One thing is said to be because it is substance, another because it is an attribute of substance, still another because it is a process toward substance, or corruption of substance, or privation of substantial forms, or quality of substance or because it produces or generates substance or that which is predicated of substance, or because it is a negation of such a thing or of substance itself. For these reasons we also say that non-being *is* non-being.

The starting point of Aristotle's doctrine of being is language—not in the way I described this starting point in neo-Platonism (hypostatization of grammatical forms, procedures and elements), but from the insight that language is predication. Hence Aristotle's focus on the copula: "Being is spoken of in many ways" because we use the copula 'is' in many contexts.

In a sense, Thomas Aquinas is still more Aristotelian in his starting point than Aristotle himself: he pushes Aristotle's realism to a point where the copula is, from the beginning, derivative of the thing's being. Let me start, therefore, with some remarks about the difference between the copula and 'being real' (what this expression means we shall have to see; but it refers to the being of the actually given sensible thing).

1. The copula and 'being real'

The copula 'is' is grounded in the reality of a thing, but it does not coincide with it.[14] This is stated in Ia 3, 4, ad 2[15] (Pegis p. 31): "'To be' can mean either of two things. It may mean the act of being, or it may mean the composition effected by the mind in joining a predicate to a subject." But these two senses of being are not equivalent. One is prior to the other. Indeed, a proposition can be formed only if a thing is given. The givenness of the thing, the reality of it, is the a priori for predications. This is stated time and again by Aquinas, for instance in this key text about truth: "In every proposition the intellect either applies to or removes from [vela applicat vel removet] the thing signified by the subject [some form signified by the predicate] [aliquam formam significatam per praedicatum]" (Ia 16, 2; Pegis p. 172). Judging thus is an operation that is measured by the reality of the thing. In speaking of the conformity theory of truth one has to keep this priority in mind: precisely this priority makes the conformity theory of truth possible. That is what it is all about: the "thing signified by the subject" of a proposition is known correctly when "the form signified by the predicate" belongs indeed to that thing. Thus when I say that the thing signified by the subject is 'heavy objects' and the forms signified by the predicate are 'scream,' something is wrong: heavy objects do not scream; they fall.

Only because of this verification in propositions can Aquinas say: "Verum secundum suam primam rationem est in intellectu" ("Truth resides, in its primary aspect, in the intellect," ibid.; Pegis p. 171). 'Primary' only because there is no conformity between thing and judgement if there is no judgement, or proposition. But, and this is essential to the entire debate, ontologically truth resides primarily in the thing: "Omnis res est vera secundum habet propriam formam naturae suae" (Pegis p. 171: "Everything is true according as it has the form proper to its nature"). Only because the thing is first of all corresponding to its nature—that is, because a given subway train does not all of a sudden produce organ music rather than run on tracks—can I articulate: the subway train runs on tracks; or, this is a subway train. "Et propter hoc per conformitatem intellectus et rei veritas definitur" ("And for this reason truth is defined by the conformity of intellect and thing"; Pegis p. 171).

The derivative character of the copula, and hence of the truth as it lies in the proposition, appears clearly from the functions of uniting and separating in judgements. I unite a predicate to a subject *in so far* as a corresponding term is united to the thing that the predicate stands for. Therefore Aquinas adds, "conformitatem istam cognoscere, est cognoscere veritatem" (To know this conformity is to know the truth; Pegis obscure here). In other words, the copula is our way of acquiescing to the conformity between the concept and the thing's reality; of stating that the identification between subject and predicate corresponds to the real state of things. The copula 'is' expresses this agreement. By the copula the discourse is about something, and goes beyond simple apprehension and comparisons.

The copula expresses two things: subjective agreement with the thing known, and the recognition by ourselves of such agreement. In the first instance we know the thing; in the second we know our knowledge to be correct. In the second case, we know the conformity; we know that what we know is true. We know that what the judgement affirms is objectively the state of affairs independently of our intellect's activity. Properly speaking, the being of the copula is a thought-thing; in this sense Thomas can say that it is "something proper" to the mind: "Ibi primo invenitur ratio veritatis, ubi primo intellectus incicipit aliquid proprium habere, quod res extra animam non habet" [the nature of truth is first found in the intellect when the intellect begins to possess something proper to itself, not possessed by the thing outside the soul] (*De Ver.* 1, 3c).[16] What the mind has as its own, and what the thing does not have, is the knowledge of correspondence which is affirmed in the copula. But what the mind possesses as its ownmost is the affirmation that the thing is: the copula answers the question: is X given? *An sit* [Whether it is]. The copula is thus *not* the being of the thing; properly speaking it is accidental to the thing. The copula differs therefore not only from the being that makes the thing real, but also from the being enunciated in all the ten categories.

Nevertheless, the relation of foundation between reality and copula is also clear: the copula is the recognition of reality. If there is no real thing, the copula has been deprived of moorage: "Ipsum esse est perfectissimum omnium, comparatur enim ad omnia ut actus. Nihil enim habet actualitatem nisi inquantum est; unde ipsum esse est actualitas omnium rerum" [being itself is the most perfect of all things, for it is compared to all things as that by which they are made actual; for nothing has actuality except so far as it is. Hence being is that which actuates all things] (not in Pegis; Ia 4, 1, ad 3).[17] It is now this idea of actuality that we have to pursue. The best entrance is again from what we have said of the copula.

2. 'Being' as being-real (actuality)

The supreme rule about judgement, the principle of non-contradiction, states that it is impossible that something be something and at the same time its contrary (Arist., *Metaph.* IV, 3; 1005 b 19). It is a principle about judgements in so far as these claim to be correct. And it says: a judgement cannot be correct if it affirms a predicate of a thing which would be contradictory to that thing.[18] Something is objectively possible only in so far as its reality can be asserted in an unconditional, generally valid contradiction to not-being. This yields a double concept of being with regard to the thing (forgetting now the copula): (1) that of which it is said that it is; Aquinas calls this 'res' [a thing] or 'aliquid' [something] or 'ens' [a being]; that which in itself is irreconcilable with not-being. (2) The being-actual itself, i.e. the respect under which something is regarded in a judgement of existence, 'actu esse' [to be in act], that which makes it that the something is unconditionally opposed to not-being. This conceptual duplicity corresponds to the duplicity of subject and predicate. That an 'ens' has 'esse' [being] is what the intellect expresses by the identification between subject and predicate. "In qualibet propositione affirmativa vera, oportet quod praedicatum et subjectum significent idem secundum rem aliquo modo, et diversum secundum rationem" (Pegis is bad here; "In every true affirmative proposition the predicate and the subject must signify in some way the same thing in reality, although from different points of view"; 1a 13, 12c).[19] The subject signifies in the thing its *ens*, the predicate its *esse*.

This allows us to understand the two basic modes of being in Thomas Aquinas—namely *ens* and *esse*. Being something and being real. An affirmative judgement of existence simply says 'X is'; it seems to be the first thing that children learn to say: 'Das da' [That there]. No comparison with other things is involved, no classification with regard to genus and species, no name even, as essence. In such an elementary judgement the subject designates that which is perceived and the predicate that as which it is perceived.

> That which is perceived = 'material object.'
> That as which it is perceived: 'formal object.'
> These have nothing to do with the distinction, matter/form.

The formal object of knowledge encompasses on the one hand all qualitative determinations of the material object, without analyzing them, and on the other hand the thing's reality. This reality means *that* the thing exists, that the material object is there. Thus Aquinas can say that 'actu esse' is "maxime formale" (Ia 7, 1: "Being is the most formal of all things," "Illud autem quod est maxime formale omnium est ipsum esse"; Pegis p. 54).

To actually be is something that cannot be defined. Whatever is, is only by such being-real or being-actual. And whatever can be known can also enter our mind only because it has being. The copula is possible for us to form because there is first of all actual reality. It is this being-real, being-actual that our mind seizes first: "Primo autem in conceptione intellectus cadit ens, quia secundum hoc unumquodque cogniscibile est, inquantum est actu" (Ia 5, 2; "The first thing conceived by the intellect is being, because every-thing is knowable only in as much as it is actually"; Pegis p. 36).

Now, how are we going to understand such utter givenness?[20] Some people have seen here an early formulation of what Kant calls being as position. Utter presence is ineffable, because whatever we would want to say would have to lean on such position, presence, actuality. Thus it can only be characterized by opposition to what is not actual.

a. Being actual[21] *vs. not being.* This is in fact what we want to say when we talk about 'actual being': that it is *not* not-being. That does not lead us very far in our conceptualization of it, however. This opposition is simply the effort to bring what is formally unconditioned into contradiction with nothingness. A contradictory opposition always bases itself upon the preliminary grasp of such positedness. "Being and nothingness are the extremes of contradictory opposition" ("Esse et non esse sunt extrema contradictionis"; De Quattuor oppositis, c. 4). But from this elementary opposition we can formulate some positive approaches of 'esse actu.'

b. Being-actual as the foundation of a thing. Indeed, as long as we grasp reality simply empirically or in things empirical, it is not the foundation of the absolute opposition to nothingness, since such an empirical thing is in itself contingent. As contingent it requires precisely such an absolute ground of positedness in order to be called contingent. Now, Aquinas calls this positedness 'actus essendi' [act of being]. In order to fully understand what is meant by 'act,' let me briefly recall what Aristotle had to say about the distinction between act and potency.

In his *Commentary on Aristotle's Metaphysics* IX, 1, Thomas Aquinas stresses the derivation of the term 'act' from 'acting,' *operatio*: "Operatio, a qua derivatum est nomen actus" [activity, from which the word 'act' is derived] (1769).[22] Or from 'movement': "Nomen actus a motu originem sumpserit, non tamen solum motus dicitur actus" [the word 'act' is derived from motion, but it is not motion alone that is designated as act] (1823). Likewise, potency originally designates the capacity to act (ibid.): "Omnes potentiae reducuntur ad aliquod principium ex quo omnes aliae dicuntur. Et hoc est principium activum, quod est principium transmutationis in alio, in quantum est aliud" [all potencies are reduced to some principle from which all the others derive their meaning; and this is an active principle, which is the source of change in some other thing in as much as it is other] (1776). Potency is here called the "principle of change." It is the capacity to act, and actuality is the carrying out of that capacity. The activity (*agere*) done is the 'actum.'[23] In other words, acts—for instance speaking—occur from time to time. We do not talk (at least most of us) without interruption. But the occasional act of speaking up requires as its ground of possibility the lasting capacity to speak up, called speech. Speech we are endowed with as a potential; speaking we perform as an act. That we are able to stage such an act has its ground in the 'potentia activa.' 'Potentia passiva' is the capacity to suffer something—for instance someone else's talkativeness.

"Dicitur potentia passiva, quae est principium, quod aliquid moveatur ab alio, in quantum est aliud" [passive potency means the principle by which one thing is moved by some other thing in as much as it is other] (*In Metaph.* IX, 1, 1777; Arist. 1019 a 15). The passive potency stands mainly in relation to being affected, 'passio.' Strictly speaking, passive potency is the capacity that a thing has to receive another form, to be determined by another— in other words, to 'become' something. So understood, passive potency applies to *all* categories: to be affected by spatial, temporal, qualitative, quantitative, relational, etc. modifications is to 'change.' "Active potency is the principle of acting upon something else, whereas passive potency is the principle of being acted upon by something else, as the Philosopher says" in *Metaph.* IV, 12; 1019 a 19 (Ia 25, 1; Pegis p. 226). The realization of passive potency is called an 'act.'

However, to stage an act, I have to be actually able to act. It may be that 'logon echein' [having speech] is an essential determination of being human, but there are individuals on earth that are unable to speak. Hence this decisive step in the appropriation of the language of *energeia* [actuality]: the primary act consists in having all that is required by the essential determination of a thing. A mute lacks the primary act of speech. The secondary act is the doing itself, the speaking up. "Actus autem est duplex, primus enim et secundus. Actum quidem primus est forma et integritas rei. Actus enim secundus est operatio" [act, however, is twofold; first, and second. The first act is the form and integrity of a thing; the second act is its operation] (Ia 48, 5; not in Pegis). The distinction between primary and secondary act corresponds in some respects to Aristotle's distinction between *dynamis* [potentiality] and *energeia* [actuality]; but these terms themselves have several meanings (see Brentano, ch. IV). I say that this distinction in Aquinas is decisive for it leads to the representation of a being that would be sheer primary act, sheer actuality, *actus purus*. In relation to the question of God's omnipotence Aquinas expands the language of actuality from that of particular qualities, e.g. speech, to that of being itself: all active potency is rooted in the primary act-to-be, actual being. Now 'to be actually' means 'to be perfect' in a thing's own order and rank: "Everything, according as it is in act and is perfect [*secundum quod est actu et perfectum*], is the active principle of something; whereas everything is passive according as it is deficient and imperfect. Now it was shown that God is pure act [*Deus est actus purus*; cf. Ia 3, 1 and 4, 1 & 2]... Whence it most fittingly belongs to him to be an active principle" and perfect (Ia 25, 1; Pegis p. 226). So the primary act = actuality or perfection of a thing; the secondary act = doing; active potency is rooted in the primary act, since "unumquodque agit secundum quod est actu" [everything acts according as it is actual] (ibid., ad 1). Thus, in this context, it is shown that God, as pure act, also possesses the utmost active potency. Passive potency, on the contrary, is for Aquinas matter: any matter in regard to the form that it is to receive, but fundamentally, prime matter.

What counts here is the sense of the primary act as that by which something is actual. The primary act is that determination that makes it that a being 'actually' is. In that sense the primary act is the foundation, or 'ground' of any thing. It does not matter here whether the being that is made real by the act coincides simply with that act (as in the case of God) or not. What counts is the step back from the couple act/potency to a more originary notion of act:[24] as the foundation of the reality of a thing, the 'act' is prior to the distinction between act and potency. As such, the act cannot be defined, it can only be elucidated by examples, analogically. Thus Aristotle says of the opposition between *energeia* [actuality] and *dynaton* [potential]: "We must not seek a definition of everything but be content to grasp the analogy, that it is as that-which-is-building to that-which-is-capable-of-building, and the waking to the sleeping, and that which is seeing to

30

that which has its eyes shut but has sight, and that which has been shaped out of the matter to the matter, and that which has been wrought up to the unwrought. Let actuality [*energeia*] be defined by one member of this antithesis, and the potential [*dynaton*] by the other" (*Metaphysics* IX, 6, 1048 a 37 ff.).

We can summarize at this point: 'act' stands simply for being-real, prior to the opposition between act and potency. Being-real as the first and primary sense of being in Aquinas is thus opposed only to being not at all. Key text for this identification between being-real and act: "Ipsum esse est perfectissimum omnium; comparatur enim ad omnia ut actus. Nihil enim habet actualitatem nisi inquantum est; unde impsum esse est actualitas omnium rerum" [being itself is the most perfect of all things, for it is compared to all things as that by which they are made actual; for nothing has actuality except so far as it exists. Hence existence is that which actuates all things] (Ia 4, 1, ad 3; not in Pegis).

'Act' answers, as I said, the question: *Is that thing? An sit?* The question 'What is it?' is answered by the essence. The act as being-real is opposed to the essence, which is secondary in that sense, as act and potency in general. Only in God, in whom there is nothing in potency, is there pure actuality. (See Ia, 3, 4; Pegis p. 31: "Being is the actuality of every form, therefore being must be compared to essence as actuality to potentiality. Therefore, since in God there is no potentiality it follows that in him essence does not differ from being," *quod non sit aliud in eo essentia quam suum esse.*) Sometimes Aquinas calls this actuality of being itself 'form.' Indeed, form is that which *gives* actuality to the composite and hence in the composite is the most real. Example: "Esse est illud quod est magis intimum cuilibet, et quod profundius omnibus inest, cum sit formale respectu omnium quae in re sunt" [being is innermost in each thing and most fundamentally inherent in all things since it is formal in respect of everything found in a thing] (Ia 8, 1; not in Pegis). Pursuing this line of reasoning one can say that being-real is received by things; it is not that which receives (Ia 4, 1, ad 3: "sicut receptum ad recipiens" [as the received to the receiver]). "When I speak of man's being, or that of a horse or anything whatsoever, that being is considered as what is formal and received [*ipsum esse consideratur ut formale et receptum*], but not as that to which being

31

is said to belong [*non autem ut illud cui competit esse*]" (ibid.). Here Aquinas distinguishes sharply between being-real and being-something: 'ipsum esse' [being itself] as actuality is that *by which* something is.

We have moved far away from Aristotle: it is clear that this distinction between being-actual and being-something, *esse* and *ens*, is only expressed in his vocabulary of form and matter, *energeia* and *dynamis*—but that the teaching is new. It indicates the conjunction of ousiology and the neo-Platonic representation of hierarchy, with a supreme being at the top: the higher one rises on the ladder of degrees, the more perfect, and that is, the more 'being,' the beings become. Aristotelian hylomorphism is only the most appropriate conceptual tool to join these two intuitions: composition and hierarchy. This is the paradigmatic case of 'expanded' Aristotelianism in the Middle Ages. Not one word is rescinded from Aristotle, but his intuitions are applied within a context that gives them (here: act and potency) a new—and probably deeper—meaning.

The being-actual is sometimes called 'quo est,' that by which something is. In this perspective—inhered from Boethius who distinguished between 'esse' [being] and 'quod est' [what is] in the case of the angels—the indistinction of being and to-be is stated: "In Deo non differt quod est et quo est" [in God what He is, and whereby He is are the same] (Ia 29, 4, ad 1).

Finally being-real, actuality, is of course not an accident as the realists of universals would have it. For a Proclus, for instance, whether a nature has being is only secondary; being for them is a predicate among others. Not so for Aquinas: *esse* constitutes the ground of a thing. But since all things exist not of themselves but as made, they have actual being 'per accidens' [accidentally]. This is one way of stating their createdness.—That much about being-real as the ground of beings. On the last three points I shall be brief:

c. Being-real as perfection. "Secundum hoc aliqua perfecta sunt, quod aliquo modo esse habent" [for things are perfect, precisely so far as they have being after some fashion] (Ia 4, 2; Pegis omits). Aquinas' notion of perfection is very peculiar. It does not mean, at least in his ontology, the Aristotelian completion, fulfillment in reaching one's natural end, *entelecheia*. Nor does it mean moral perfection as victory over evil. Rather one could describe it as a 'quality.' One speaks of 'a' perfection in a thing. Goodness, truth, etc. are 'transcendental perfections.' God as possessing all qualities is 'perfectio omnimoda' [perfect in every way]. Now, the primary perfection of a thing is 'to be.' All other perfections are either convertible with *esse* (the transcendentals) or dependent on it (accidents).

Being-real, actuality, is the most perfect of all perfections since of itself (*in sua ratione formali* [in its formal account]) it does not negate any other perfection. Only insofar as something participates in being-real can it also be said to be in any way perfect. But as such utter perfection it is in itself indeterminate—at least in non-divine beings. Hence it requires essence to receive determination, further perfections. The idea of utter perfection is thus not opposed to that of finitude or composition: the being-character of a thing is its utter perfection. That does not exclude that this being is received, participated from a cause. In as much as that utter perfection is indeterminate in itself and requires determination, it is contingent.

d. Being-real as infinite. Since in actuality qua actuality there are no differences, the act of being is, formally speaking, not finite: "Esse autem participatum finitur ad capacitatem participantis" [participated being is limited by the capacity of the participator] (Ia 75, 5, ad 4; not in Pegis). Only in God is this *esse* pure and infinite; but its nature is to be so; it is restricted, rendered finite only by that in which the act is received. Thus Aquinas does not want to say, of course, that being-real considered apart is infinite (i.e. only in God), but rather that being-real, actuality, cannot limit itself. Of itself it has no differentiation. It is not the principle of finitude. Finite comes from elsewhere, from 'essence.' The same thing can be said of the other perfections: considered absolutely, life for instance cannot negate life, nor can it limit life; otherwise it would stand in contradiction with itself.

Only because these perfections, and first of all being, do not subsist by themselves are they finite, limited. If life were to be by itself, and not in that orangutan or that roach, it would be perfect, and not limited to fists banging on a chest or crawling on six legs over a kitchen board. Being real 'as such,' and not only in God, is said to be infinite by Aquinas because out of itself it comprises no limitation under any respect.

e. Being-real as simple. Finally, from the absolute incompatibility between being-real and not-being follows the simplicity of being. This is clear now: actuality as actuality cannot be composed, complex; otherwise there would be differences within the very concept of reality; there would be some third between being-real and not-being, and being-real would negate itself. The contradictory opposition between being and not-being is indivisible, Aquinas says.

Of itself, then, being-real means the most formal identity and simplicity even when, the way it is realized in a given being, it is of course not simple but enters into a composite. Thus here again, the simplicity we are talking about is not 'ontic'; it is not the simplicity of this or that being. Rather it is ontological in the sense of a determination present in all beings, created or uncreated. It rests on the formal contradictory opposition to not-being.

After these remarks on actuality, or *esse*, or being-real, we now have to see the sense of being as 'being a thing,' *ens nominaliter sumptum* [being taken as a noun] ... i.e. 'ens' as opposed to 'esse.' This is not 'essence' (we shall not speak directly of essence), but the composite of *esse* and essence.

3. 'Being' as being a thing

What is a thing?[25] That of which actuality is predicable. We say 'X is' and thus predicate being-real of something. A thing is "id cuius actus est esse" [that whose act is being] (*De natura generis*, ch. I). In Ia 48, 2, ad 2 (not in Pegis) Aquinas calls this thingness 'entitas' [beingness] and he adds: "et sic convertitur cum re" [and in that sense it is convertible with thing]. *Entitas* translates *ousia*. He also says: thingness is that which properly is, 'quod est,' as opposed to that by which it is, 'quo est,' namely act. Most frequent names used: *ens, res, aliquid*.

Being-a-thing has to be cover all that there is, if it is a concept as large as the definition 'id cuius actus est esse' implies. Furthermore, we have to see whether it coincides with 'essence' or not, since both essence and being-a-thing are said to differ from actuality. Finally, we have to relate it to actuality, or being. Thus three points here: the scope of being-a-thing, its relation to essence, its relation to being.

a. The scope of 'being-a-thing.' To summarize this inquiry right away: everything, from God to accidents, is said to be a thing, in Aquinas. Every thing is a being, *ens*. But not in the same sense. First Aquinas follows Aristotle in distinguishing the being-a-thing in substance from the being-a-thing of accidents.

Commenting on Book V of the *Metaphysics* Aquinas distinguishes 'ens per se,' that which is a being by itself, from 'ens per accidens,' that which is a being accidentally. However, this distinction does not exactly coincide with that between substance and accidents: in the large sense both substance and accidents are 'beings by themselves.' Here 'accidental' means not forming a whole such as accident and substance do. 'Ens per accidens' is, for instance, Einstein's musical talent. Accidentally two or more determinations— being a physicist and being a violinist—come together into a unity which is not necessary, but by chance. Between being a physicist and being a violinist there is no essential link. Thomas states this in saying: there is no common cause to physicist-violinist. "Omne quod est per se habet causam, quod enim est per accidens, non habet causam" [everything that is a being per se, has a cause; but what is accidentally, has not a cause] [Ia 115, 6]. This would be unintelligible if 'per se' meant 'substantially' and 'per accidens' 'accidentally.' The rest of the text shows that 'per se' is said also of accidents, here 'being white' and 'being a musician': "Album enim causam habet, similiter et musicum; sed album musicum non habet causam, quia non est vere ens neque vere unum" [for (that a thing) is *white* has a cause, likewise (that a man is) *musical* has a cause, but (that a being is) *white-musical* has not a cause, because it is not truly a being, not truly one] (Ia 115, 6; not in Pegis).

What forms a unity of being only by coincidence does not deserve the title 'being' or 'thing'; it is not an object for science.

The 'ens per se' not only includes, then, substance and accidents, but also the 'ens rationis,' thought-objects. One such thought object is the copula, although, as I have said, it is grounded in reality. Primarily being a thing is said of real beings, the sensible substance.

The scope of being-a-thing, i.e. of predicamental being, can be determined out of the terms subordinated under the ten categories.

aa) Substance and categories. On this point again Thomas follows Aristotle quite closely, so that I do not have to explain this doctrine in detail. The categories are the supreme predicaments of what he calls the 'first substance,' i.e. the real thing, the sensible object. The categories differ from one another by their relation to that first substance (on this point, in Aristotle—with a somewhat Thomist view—see Brentano, ch. V).

'First substance' is what we would call the individual. Thomas has several expressions for this: *suppositum* [supposit, literally that which is placed under], subsistence, hypostasis, *quod est*, *res*. A *suppositum* endowed with reason is called a person. The *hypokeimenon* [underlying thing], Thomas says, is translated as 'subjectum vel suppositum' [subject or supposit], i.e. "quod subsistit in genere substantiae" [what subsists in the genus of substance]. Now this has three further names: "In as much as it exists by itself and not by another it is called 'subsistentia' [subsistence]; indeed, we say that those things subsist which exist not in something other but by themselves. Secondly, in as much as it is placed under some common nature it is called 'res naturae' [a thing of nature]; this particular man, for instance, is a thing of human nature. Thirdly, in as much as it is placed under the accidents, it is called 'hypostasis vel substantia' [hypostasis, or substance]. Now, what these three terms designate generally in all that is substantial, the term 'persona' designates in all that is both substantial and endowed with reason" (Ia 29, 2; not in Pegis).

'First substance' or 'individual' is thus an empirical concept: it designates what we encounter first, that which 'falls' first into our experience (simple apprehension). Experience as described by Aquinas is thus irreducibly multifarious: "this empirical datum is not that one—*hoc ens non est illud ens.*" "What first comes to the intellect is being [*quod primo cadit in intellectu ens*]; secondly that this being is not that being, and thus we apprehend division as a consequence [*et sic secundo apprehendimus divisionem*]; thirdly comes the notion of one, and fourthly the notion of multitude" (Ia 11, 2, 4m; Pegis p. 66). These ingredients of experience center around individual beings as the bearer for all statements that apply to reality. This stress on individuation, which entails ontological autonomy, is what characterizes most deeply the new achievement of philosophy in medieval neo-Aristotelianism. Individuality is an ultimate ontological datum. It means, in fact, two things: the autonomous individual thing is the ultimate bearer of its predicamental determinations; and: such an autonomous individual is opposed to the multitude of all other such individuals. "Substantia individuatur per seipsam" [substance is individualized by itself] (Ia 29, 1; not in Pegis). The thing is as wide as its act extends: it acts itself, is not acted upon; it posits its own act; it has the "dominium sui actus" [dominion over its action] (ibid.). "Individuum est quod est in se indistinctum, ab aliis vero distinctum" [the individual in itself is undivided, but is distinct from others] (Ia 29, 4). The thing as individual does not inhere in anything. That is what is meant by 'subsistence': the thing is a totality, fully rounded in itself, which has its principle of being in itself and thus 'subsists' by itself.

Thomas goes very far in this praise of the autonomy of what he calls the first substance: it is incommunicable: "substantiae individuae, id est distinctae et incommunicabiles" [the individual— i.e., distinct and incommunicable substance] (Ia 29, 4, ad 3). This incommunicability is given with subsistence, so that subsistence can be said to make up the essence of the first substance as individual. Accidents are those determinations of the individual substance that do not 'constitute' it but 'befall' it. The individual substance individualizes the accidents. Accidents inhere in the first substance; their being is 'esse in alio' [being in another].

'Second substances' are the species and genera, i.e. the content of general substantial determinations predicable of many individuals. The second substance is a predicate of the first substance; it determines the first substance as 'animal' and 'ratio' determine Socrates. The highest genus, the highest such secondary substance, is the very category of substance

bb) The categories are things, too; however, not in the strict sense. Commenting on Aristotle Aquinas says: "The substance is a being purely and simply, whereas all other categories, which differ from substance, are beings [entia] only in a certain rapport and by the substance" (*In Metaph.* VII, 1 (1248)). "The first substance is what is in the proper sense, primarily, and most substance" (ibid. 1274). "Illi enim proprie convenit esse, quod habet esse, et quod est subsistens in suo esse" [for being belongs to that which has being—that is, to what subsists in its own being] (Ia 45, 4; not in Pegis). Only the substance properly has actual being, but "forms and accidents and other such things [!, R.S.] are not called 'entia' as if they were by themselves but since through them something is [*quia eis aliquid est*]." This last formulation can be misunderstood: by no means does Aquinas want to say that the accidents have a kind of causality upon the substance; the text shows that clearly: "Thus whiteness is called a being for the simple reason that through it a subject is white" (ibid.). Whereas everything else subsists only through a first substance, the first substances subsist by themselves. First substances or individuals are then things properly speaking, "ens [res, R.S.] nominaliter sumptum" [being [thing] taken as a noun].

Secondary substances—species and genera—are 'things' not properly speaking. Otherwise the concept of being, *ens*, would be a supreme genus, encompassing all secondary substances, too. But, "As the Philosopher shows in *Metaph.* III, 8, 'ens non potest esse genus alicuius'" [being cannot be a genus] (1a 3, 5; not in Pegis). Rather the secondary substances are abstracted from the primary of first substances. The generic concept so obtained however has to be predicated also of the specific difference and of individuations such as accidental. A difficulty arises then with regard to the concept of being. It must belong both to the contents of general concepts such as genera and to the individual substances. But these individual substances exclude predicability of being many things: they are always 'this or that.' Thus the concept of being seems to imply a formal contradiction: said both of what is general as general, and of the individual as individual. But we would have such a contradiction only if the concept of being were univocal.

Aquinas follows Aristotle in saying that all modalities of the concept of being-a-thing—i.e. accidents, primary substance, secondary substance—are derived from the primary substance. Only of this, then, will being-real be predicated. Analogy, here (later something else) means this reference to that which is a being primarily, namely the individual, subsisting thing.

Thus accidents cannot properly be called beings, but rather 'beings of beings,' *entis entia*. Best translation perhaps: 'determinations' of things. The accidents "are said to be beings, not as though they themselves were subsistents, but because through them other things are beings... [T]hus whiteness is not said to be a being because it exists in anything else, but because, by it, something else has accidental being, namely, a thing that is white" (Ia 5, 5, ad 2; Pegis p. 43). Accidents determine a subsisting thing in this or that fashion; theirs is an 'ens quo' [a being by which] not an 'ens quod' [a being which]. They are 'entia' insofar as they can be predicated of the first substance. "Quia accidentia non videntur entia prout secundum se significantur, sed solum prout significantur in concretione ad substantiam, patet quod singula aliorum entium sunt entia propter substantiam" [since accidents do not seem to be beings in so far as they are signified in themselves, but only in so far as they are signified in connection with substance, evidently it is by reason of this that each of the other beings is a being] (*In Metaph.* VII, 1, 1256). "Accidens non habet subsistentiam nisi ex subiecto" [accidents subsist only in a subject] (ibid.). The same relation is said of the parts of a substance: they, too, are 'ens quo.' But they partake more closely of substantial being, since they are precisely parts of the substance.

cc) We can now determine the notion of being-a-thing, *ens ut sic* [a being as such]. We have seen that it cannot be a univocal concept, since it is said of genera, species, individuals, and individuated accidents. In univocal concepts the same word is said of different things in the same sense. The concept of *ens* is analogical for the reason stated: all *entia* are spoken of in reference to the primary substance. The primary substance is 'ens ut sic' in its proper sense. The notion of being-a-thing thus covers all that can be predicated of a primary substance. By this primary substance all other types of 'things' can be said to be actual. Such is the elementary participation: by belonging to a subsisting thing, other things receive their actuality (although not their being-a-thing as the text on whiteness just quoted indicates).

Both *ens* and *esse* are predicable of God: he is *Ipsum esse* [Being Itself], and *summum ens* [the highest being]. However, they can be so predicated only in an analogical fashion, which differs from the substantial analogy just mentioned. This for later. The *analogia entis* [analogy of being] in this domain will have to express the infinite distance between fully being and being composite, and at the same time the fact that *ens* and *esse* are predicable positively of God, that they belong to him 'proprie' [properly].

To conclude these remarks on the scope of 'being-a-thing,' it is clear that 'ens' is a derivate (present participle and noun) of *esse*, the verb. The inner simplicity of a fully rounded thing stems ultimately from the actual being, from the simplicity of being-actual. Thus the most appropriate definition of being-a-thing is to say that it is "that whose act is to-be," *Id cuius actus est esse* (*De natura generis*, ch. I). But before looking at that relation between being-a-thing and being-real, we have to look at 'essence.'

b. *'Being a thing' and essence.* The fundamental opposition is that between *esse* and *ens*, being actual or real and being a thing. There are texts where this fundamental opposition is expressed as that between existence and essence. I now want to show that there is a proportionality

$$\frac{esse}{ens} \qquad \frac{existence}{essence}$$

but that the second couple restricts what the first contains—in other words, *essentia* [essence] is a partial determination of 'ens.'

In the primary, elementary, act of 'simple apprehension' we grasp a total something out there. We 'hit upon' a thing, i.e. 'ens.' But we apprehend it *as* something. In the simple apprehension of something *as* something, we grasp its essence; we recognize things for what they are in our world. The difference between 'ens' and 'essence' is that between a universe of things and a universe of things recognizable. Experiences such as the one described in Sartre's *Nausea*, where a tree trunk seems irretrievably alien, could be described as the passage from a world of beings recognized in their essence, to a world of beings deprived of their essences. The 'ti estin' [what is] in such an experience is lost—but not the 'on' [being]. This suggests the difference between 'ens' and essence.

Both the Greek 'ousia' and the Latin 'essentia' are derived from the verb 'to be.'[26] For an Aristotelian and Thomistic mind, they suggest only a determination upon the existing thing: that aspect according to which it is knowable. What we know about a thing is its essence. According to Aristotle, we know a thing by its form. But 'form,' in Aquinas, says still less than 'essence': the form is that which gives being to a thing, whereas the 'essence' encompasses the secondary substances of species and genus. So: 'ens' says more than 'essence,' namely the fully existing thing; and 'essence' says more than 'form,' namely the universal (or secondary substance) as realized in a thing. The form is that aspect of a thing which realizes the essence.

In its technical sense, the concept of essence, then, considers a thing in its abstract determination expressed by the definition. The concept of essence disregards, not only the 'act,' but also the individual determinations, i.e. accidents. But even in this technical sense, the concept of essence is not simple: when you hear someone say, 'treat me as a human being,' two things are meant: 'homo' and 'humanitas'; I as a human being, and humanity in general, abstractly. The first, 'man,' is the concrete essence, the second, 'humanity,' the specific essence. To call both 'essentia' is properly an ontological way of speaking: the concrete human being, 'on,' has but the same title as the abstract or specific being, expressed by the definition, 'logos.' Ontology is, literally taken, the title for pre-Cartesian metaphysics: the title for the unity of conceptual and entitative determinations. This unity appears most clearly in Aquinas' understanding of essence as that which determines the thingness of a thing as well as its concept (by the definition). The title 'ontology' synthesizes constitution and definition.

"Definitio ratio est significans quod quid est" [a definition is an intelligible expression signifying a quiddity] (In Metaph., VII, 12, 1537). "The essence or nature includes only what falls within the definition of the species [i.e., it does not include actuality or the accidents, R.S.]; as humanity includes all that falls within the definition of man, for it is by this that man is man, and it is this that humanity signifies, that, namely, whereby man is man" (Ia 3, 3; Pegis p. 29). This quote shows very beautifully the ontological realism of Aquinas: the essence is said to correspond, on the one hand,

41

to "illa quae cadunt in definitione speciei" [what falls within the definition of the species] and on the other hand to "hoc quo homo est homo," that by which a (concrete) man is a man. The first expresses the 'logos' in the title 'ontology,' the second the 'on.'

The relation between thing and essence should then be clear: the essence is responsible for what the thing is, and it is expressed in the definition. In that sense it is coextensive with 'nature': "essentia uniuscuiusque rei, quam significat eius definitio, vocatur natura" [the essence of anything, signified by the definition, is commonly called nature] (Ia 29, 1, ad 4; not in Pegis). More strictly, however, 'nature' designates the essence in so far as it is the principle of action (ibid.); on this point Aquinas quotes from Aristotle: a natural thing "has within itself its principle of motion and stationariness" (*Physics* II, 1; 192 b 14). The Greek 'physis' [nature] as well as the Latin 'natura' indicate this origin in the context of motion: "nomen naturae primo impositum est ad significandam 'generationem viventium,' quae dicitur nativitas" [the word *nature* was first used to signify the generation of living things, which is called nativity] (Ia 29, 1, ad 4).

For the sake of simplification, one can say that the distinction between 'ens' and essence is merely logical. In reality essence and thing, concrete whatness and the object of simple apprehension, coincide. Only logically is there a distinction between what is perceived (*ens*) and 'as what' it is perceived (essence); this logical distinction then articulates the fact that 'ens' is the ground for subsistence, whereas 'essentia' is the ground for the inner constituents that make the thing what it is. Quite often, Thomas designates 'being-a-thing' simply by 'essence.' So, the distinction between 'ens' and 'essentia' is only logical; but the distinction between 'ens' and 'esse' is real. Let me, then, briefly conclude on this single most radical distinction in Aquinas.

c. 'Being a thing' and 'being actual.' This relation can be spelled out into three directions, according to the three notions of 'act,' namely 'act' as opposed to potency, as opposed to a potential being, and as opposed to a being in potentiality. The first distinction is taken from the Aristotelian analysis of accidental change; the second from that of substantial change, or generation and corruption; and the third from the debate against the holders of universalist realism.

aa) 'Being a thing' as potency. From the way all this began—Aquinas' usage of Aristotle's distinction between whatness and thatness—it is clear that the act 'actualizes' being-a-thing. However, this is exact only approximately: the constituted thing is the composite of actuality and thingness; it is 'the actual thing'; properly speaking, the act actualizes the essence. The precise way of expressing oneself is: the thing is the 'subject' of the act. 'Ens est cuius actus est esse' [a being is that whose act is being]: the relation between *ens* and *actus* is that between substratum, or subject, and predicate.

bb) It is clear from this that one cannot say that the thing is a potential being the way one says that the 'end' of substantial change is a potential being as long as the change, or generation (or corruption) is not completed. Even in the seed, actuality and thingness come together; to say that the tree is a potential being of the seed, is speaking of it in another perspective. The thing designates, not that which 'can,' but the enduring element in that which really is, i.e. in the object of our simple apprehension.

cc) Finally, it is also clear that the thingness does not designate a potential being such as a thought-object. The essence corresponds to such thought-objects, but the 'res' [thing] is always something real. And even if we call a delirium a 'res,' it is real as delirium. This impossibility of reducing the 'ens' to a version of 'dynamis' [potentiality] only shows again what I said at the beginning about 'energeia' [actuality] and the 'actus essendi' [act of being]: namely that Aquinas' concept of actuality steps back from the Aristotelian couple act/potency to uncover an actuality in things to which a polar potentiality does not correspond.

This distinction between being-actual and being-a-thing shows the ways that Aquinas follows in order to establish the autonomy of the sensible substance. In a historical perspective, this recognition of substantial autonomy is only one step—although a decisive one—in the desacralization of the world (which, in religious

43

terms, is an entirely Jewish concept). The Western tradition, to do justice to the chief injunction of the Jewish God: 'Do not confuse me with the universe,'[27] had to go through a long process of disentangling substantial autonomy and cohesion through participation. Descartes, Kant, positivism, etc., are just as many steps that take this recognition of mundane autonomy further. But compared to the neo-Platonic tradition, this recognition begins with Aquinas. I now want to show how this recognition of the autonomy of beings is at the heart of Aquinas' concept of analogy between the Creator and the created.

4. Aquinas' concept of analogy

a. Reminder of Aristotle's concept of analogy.[28] Aristotle explains the guiding principle of his theory of analogy at the beginning of the *Physics* where he refutes the Eleatic doctrine of the unicity of being: "being is spoken of in several ways" (*Physics* I, 2; 185 a 21). It is a matter of observation that man speaks of being, 'on,' on multiple occasions. What can also be observed are the manifold instances to which this word applies. Thus Aristotle's starting point is human speech, and particularly the copula 'is.' In the *Categories* he submits a list of the ten main ways of using the term 'to be' (IV; 1 b 25). The first step, in Aristotle, thus consists in establishing the multiple ways of speaking about being.

The second step is also based on observation: the many ways to speak of being are not irreducible to one another. The ten acceptations of the verb 'to be' are enumerated according to an order: the first among them, being as *ousia*, substance, remains the reference in relation to which the nine others are defined. This 'denominative' reference to a primordial acceptation is stated in the *Metaphysics*: "Being is spoken of in several ways, but always with reference to a single term, a single nature, and not homonymously."[29] Aristotle did not give a name to this unity of order by reference to a first, but it is circumscribed by a paraphrase: *pollachōs legetai, alla pros hen*: "in several ways, but in reference to one." Logically then, each time the word *on* is used, a relationship is established between being as substance and the nine other meanings of the copula.[30]

This is Aristotle's second observation. In these texts, the term *analogia* is never mentioned with regard to the doctrine of being. Later, the Arabic Aristotelians translate the relation to a first, *pros* [in reference to], by the word "attribute"; and two centuries after Meister Eckhart, Cajetan speaks of an analogy of attribution in order to designate the unity between the secondary and primary acceptations of the word 'being,' that is, the unity between accidents and substance. Aristotle has hardly explained either the conditions of *pros* or those of the ground and foundation which the substance provides for dispositions, actions, and movements that affect it.

One would be mistaken to confuse the 'first' with some real universal entity. For Aristotle *ousia* designates the individual substance, the subject of all determinations. Beyond this substance as subject there is *no* avenue for seeking a single cosmic foundation. Being as *ousia* is not numerically one. The notion of being is one and universal only insofar as it refers to an intelligible. "The universal is either nothing or it follows from existing singulars."[31] The question of the unicity of a primordial substance (such as the "sphere" in Parmenides), to which the word *on* would be applied by priority, remains in suspension. The multiplicity of substances appears impossible to overcome; only their predicates are thought of in an analogous relationship. This is the third phase.

b. Models of analogy in Aquinas. The fourth and last step was taken more than a thousand years after Aristotle. It consists in applying the predicamental analogy to the relationship between the created and the uncreated. To Aristotle, such a broadening of his doctrine would have been properly incomprehensible. In medieval Aristotelianism beings are seen in a relation to God which closely resembles some aspects of the relation between substance and accidents. On the one hand, if creation entailed a complete break between the Creator and the creature, the demands of philosophy as well as those of faith would be contradicted. Truth can be communicated from God to man only on the basis of a communication of being. If, on the other hand, God dissolved into the cosmos to form one single substance with it, the very principle of creation would dissolve at the same time.

In his Commentary on the *Sentences*[32] Thomas distinguishes between three types of analogy: the first is called according to concept, but not according to being *(secundum intentionem tantum)*. The case of 'health' traditionally illustrates this first acceptation: health is in the organism, but it has no common being with the blood tested or food, although these too can be called 'healthy.' The second kind of analogy is according to being, but not according to concept *(secundum esse et non secundum intentionem)*. Thomas cites as an example the 'body' whose concept is univocally applied to celestial, imperishable bodies and to animal bodies, which are perishable. In these cases 'body' designates realities whose being does not fall under the same genus. Thirdly, an analogy can be both according to concept and to being *(secundum intentionem et secundum esse)*. This latter type brings together under one name a determination of being that is present to all entities derived from the first, but which the inferior participants realize by mode of a diminished perfection. The concept possesses its full significance only in the first member of the analogy, that which all other members participate but which itself participates nothing. In this way, truth and goodness are found both in God and in the created; they are attributed analogically to what is fully true and good as well as to what is only partly true and good.

In his treatise *On Truth*[33] Thomas calls this kind of agreement between the two terms a 'proportion.' *Proportio* was the word by which Boethius had translated *analogia*. A proportion is a determined relationship between two concrete terms. It concerns primarily substance and accident. The difficulty with Boethius' expression stems from the incomparable, literally disproportionate, greatness of God when compared to things created: there is no common 'proportion' between the finite and the infinite. Thomas prefers, therefore, a scheme of analogy that unites not two, but four members. The relation is established between two different proportionate attributions of the same term—"between two related proportions," says the text. The physical eye 'sees,' but intelligence, too, 'sees.' Yet the vision that is proportionate to the physical eye is quite different from the vision that is proportionate to the intellect. Some names taken from the domain of the created can be attributed to

God according to the same procedure. Formally, such an analogy of proportionality states that A is to B as C is to D.

Neither the solution of the Commentary on the *Sentences* nor that of *On Truth* seems however to allow for real continuity between the two terms of analogy. In his *Summa Theologiae* Thomas proposes a third way of approaching the problem.[34] Here the analogy is drawn between two or more secondary terms and a first one which precedes and includes them (*duorum respectu tertii* [of two with respect to a third]). An ape's intelligence and a human's intelligence can be compared only under the heading of a third term, Intelligence itself. Since neither the ape nor man realizes intelligence perfectly, Thomas finally proposes an analogy in which one of the two terms is strictly first (*unius ad alterum* [of one to the other]). Only in such a type of analogy is there a real communication between the uncreated and the created, as the created is referred directly to its cause. It is this kind of analogy that introduces Aristotelianism into theodicy. Indeed, it applies to the relations between substance and accident, but also to those between God and the world. God infinitely and in fullness possesses the attributes which the creature appropriates in a finite mode through participation. You see how this rationality of creation goes back in a straight line to Aristotle's predicamental analogy. It allows us to trace the perfections observed in things back into the very being of God. The perfections are the same in the created as in the Creator; they differ only by their mode of realization.

c. Analogy and act.[35] Much of what Aquinas says about participation of perfections could be appropriated in a neo-Platonic view. A neo-Platonic philosophy of the hierarchy of beings located things inanimate, animate and rational precisely according to the degrees to which they share in divine qualities such as being, life, intelligence. And in each rank of beings these qualities are captured, so to speak, according to limited, i.e. deficient, similarity.

Aquinas' originality consists in the preeminence that he gives to the act. He says of the degrees of goodness, for instance: "Goodness is spoken of as more or less according to a superadded actuality" (Ia 5, 1, ad 3; Pegis p. 36; *bonum dicitur secundum magis et minus, secundum actum supervenientem*). 'Supervenire' [To superadd] is here a technical term to indicate that of itself a perfection is nothing unless it is rendered real by actuality. Actuality, Aquinas says in a metaphorical way, is what all things desire. Their qualities, whatever they may be, depend on their act-to-be. Now, the argument that is meant to show this priority of act in the schemes of participation hinges again on the couple act/potency: in order to participate in something, a being has to be towards that something in a state of potency (man's participation in rationality indicates that the animal is rational potentially); now, actuality is by definition the very negation of potency; hence actuality participates, as actuality, in nothing.

"Ipsum esse [Being itself] is the most perfect of all [*perfectissimum omnium*]; indeed, it is the actuality of everything. No being has actuality unless it be; hence *ipsum esse* is the actuality of all things... It must not be called a recipient, but that which is received. Thus when I speak of man's or a horse's being 'ipsum esse consideratur ut receptum' [being itself is considered as something received]; but being is not understood as that to which 'esse' is added" (Ia 4, 1, ad 3; not in Pegis).

Avicenna taught something similar, which turns out, however, to stand at the opposite extreme of Aquinas' intentions. Avicenna had interpreted Aristotle's 'nous poiētikos' [active intellect] in the sense that one Active Intellect grants actuality to all things and actually is present in all things. Aquinas' theory, on the other hand, never implies a unicity of act. He says that God is 'ipsum esse' [being itself] and 'actus purus' [pure act], but at the same time he sees the actuality of things created as entirely theirs: so much so that positing an act is understood by him as an activity—'actus exercitus' [an act performed]. Aquinas, in seeing actuality as the primary realm of participation intends the exact opposite of a deification of the world: as if wherever there is actuality, there is God who is pure actuality. No, the very term 'actuality' or 'act' is introduced by him to affirm the autonomy of the created. It is an essence that limits the act in infinite numbers of ways, thus producing indeed a world of unequal layers, but in which each layer, each being, receives from the first principle only its capacity to produce its act. Thus Aquinas has recognized the originality of the 'esse' [being] both with regard to 'ens' [beings] and to God. One should not even call the *esse*

48

'positedness,' as I have done, since it is rather an auto-positing. Existence is not conceived as a fact, but as an act.

At the same time, of course, the act is integrated into the scheme of analogy in such a way that Aquinas can say: human reason, even without belief, can discover this dependence. To hold a philosophy that would imply that there is anything whatsoever that does not depend on God, is an abominable error of reason (*De aeternitate mundi*, Vivès XXVII, 450). The metaphysics of 'analogia entis' [analogy of being] is meant to allow us to hold at the same time the act's createdness and its autonomy. It is created, participated, i.e. dependent in as much as actuality in general, qua actuality, would not be if the pure act, i.e. God, were not; but it is autonomous in so far as God gives to each being the power to posit its own act.

A quote from Aristotle, frequently used by Aquinas in this context, illustrates what is meant by the simultaneous dependency and autonomy: "first is the hottest of things; for it is the cause of the heat of all other things" (*Metaph.* II, 1; 993 b 25). Aquinas paraphrases: "Id quod est maxime ens est causa omnis entis" [whatever is greatest in being is the cause of every being] (Ia 44, 1; not in Pegis). Once a tree-trunk burns, it burns by itself; likewise "Deus est ipsum esse per se subsistens" [God is self-subsisting being itself], but once another thing has 'caught' the actuality as wood catches fire, it has its own act. Aquinas speaks of the "received act," which nevertheless, once received, is my own; whereas a scheme of reception of qualities never allows one to view these qualities as really mine the act is—because it does not contain 'more or less'—really mine.

Thus things created are radically dependent—since 'to-be,' *esse*, is the very core of any thing, as has been shown—and radically autonomous.[36] Indeed, the pure act of being is in all beings, but without swallowing them up, without becoming these beings. This is thinkable because the pure act is actually nothing, not a thing, not an *ens*, not a predicate. As the utter actuality of all that is actual, the pure act can be in things without altering anything of their individuality. As sheer actuality it can communicate itself to all things without alienating either itself in them, or them in it.

The communication of actuality would be merely logical if it were conceived on the model of inclusion: towards larger and larger genera. But the vocabulary of act takes ontology altogether out of such a metaphysics of inclusion or even of hierarchy: thus it preserves the plurality of individuals. Whatever participates the act, possesses its own consistency. If the notion of being were univocal, there would be no real otherness in the universe. If it were equivocal, there would be no communication in the world. Now, if there is a communication of actuality which at the same time preserves the otherness of Creator and creature, the concept of being here is analogical.

The act is communicated in such a way that 'being-a-thing' limits it by its perfections. But the actuality as primary perfection is the bearer of all these other perfections, general or individual. We can therefore consider actuality in two ways, in things: qua actuality, it is always pure, infinite, as has been said. But as realized, it is mixed, limited, finite. Aquinas uses both types of expressions.

You can see again how this notion of analogy of act allows Aquinas to think the diversity of beings. They are utterly manifold, but not irreducibly so, since they all are actual. Things that stand in a relation of analogy to one another are "secundum rationes partim diversae, partim non diversae" [according to means which are partly different and partly not] [cf. *In Metaph*. IV, 1 (535)]. They are diverse: they have multifarious ways of relating to the first, to the actuality in them; they are not diverse: the terminus of all these relations is the same, namely the pure act. Things stand to pure act "secundum diversae habitudines" [according to different relationships], but they stand all in relation to the pure act, hence "ad unum et idem" [to one and the same]. The pure act is properly speaking the 'principle' of analogical relations.

II.

Aquinas' Philosophy of Knowledge

It is out of the question to present the very elaborate philosophy of knowledge here, as contained, e.g., in questions of the *Summa*. See for instance Karl Rahner, *Spirit in the World*, for the role of 'phantasmata' [images] in abstraction. Here I want to address myself only to what constitutes the core of Aquinas' philosophy of knowledge. This can be stated briefly: actuality as what is common to the knower and the known constitutes the common 'nature' of knower and known. Hence knowledge is called 'connatural.' This ground of connaturality precedes actual knowledge or knowledge by 'adaequatio' [equating].

1. Knowledge as secondary act

In presenting the vocabulary of act, we saw that the notion of 'actus essendi' [act of being, act 'to be'] in Aquinas has no precedent in Aristotle, since there is no potentiality correlated to the actuality of 'esse' [being, to be].[37] That is why one had to speak of actuality as the 'ground,' core, etc., of beings. And that is why actuality as such appeared utterly simple, literally infinite. Aquinas speaks of the single actuality in all beings: "actualitas omnium rerum" (1a, 4, 1, ad 3; not in Pegis). For an Aristotelian mind, this notion of actuality, deprived of a correlated potentiality, is unintelligible. We therefore have to distinguish two notions of 'act':

- primary act: the act 'to be,' which is said even of things potential;
- secondary act: contingency, an act that can cease and which cancels a potentiality.

The primary act is said even of things potential: "Those things which are not purely and simply, nevertheless 'are' in a certain sense... Those that do not exist actually, exist potentially [*ea quae non sunt actu, sunt in potentia*]" (Ia 14, 9; mixed up in Pegis p. 143). 'Sunt'

[Are] potentially: the central notion of 'esse' underlies both things actual and things potential in the narrow sense. In this sense every potency is an act-to-be. Even of prime matter Aquinas says that it somehow participates in actuality: "aliquo modo est, quia est ens in potentia" [in some way is, for it is potentially a being] (*Contra Gentiles*, 2, 16). At the same time, he can also say of prime matter, since it is formless, that it is nothing, "non ens."

The secondary act is "vertibile in nihilum" [changeable into nothing] (Ia 75, 6, ad 2; Pegis p. 289)—Aquinas' phrase for what is contingent. Things contingent are 'entia' [beings] in the broadest sense indicated previously, including activities. The secondary act is mostly described as such an activity: 'agere sequitur esse' [acting follows being]. Contingency, potentiality, 'vertibile in nihilum,' designate the element of not-being in the secondary act of being. But in the 'actuality' as primary act there is no such element of non-being. There is no 'more or less' of being in utter actuality. Only of the secondary act can one say that being is 'weak,' for instance (said of prime matter, *De Ver.* 3, 5, ad 1). Actuality as such cannot be determined by finitude. It is, of course, only a point of view upon things: "actus entis inquantum est ens" [the act of a being in so far as it is a being] (*Quodl.* 9, 2, 2). But this 'inquantum' [in so far as] makes knowledge possible:

– pure actuality = common ground of knower and known = ontological truth
– finite act = content of a true judgement = ontic truth

The pure actuality is what all things have in common, whether created or not. Thus a common ground pervades the universe, in Aquinas' view, which makes knowledge possible. This is already knowledge: by connaturality. The finite act, on the other hand, requires labor in order for knowledge to be obtained: abstraction, 'composition and division' …

This opposition between 'knowledge by connaturality' and 'knowledge by conformity' is what we have to elucidate now. It parallels the opposition between pure actuality and finite act. One could also call it the difference between originary knowledge and objective knowledge. Connatural knowledge is originary since it is said to belong to the 'nature' of all things; it founds the 'desiderium naturale videndi Deum' [natural desire to see God]. Knowledge by conformity is objective since it requires an object (taken literally: *ob-jacere* [to throw in the way of]) to be present in order for a proposition of the mind to be correct. You see the pre-modern notion of object: objectivity is *not* the being of objects. The being of all things, prior to the distinction between subject and object, is 'esse.' To connatural knowledge things show themselves of themselves. Connatural knowledge is a basic communication, acquaintance with all things, including God. Aquinas does not draw any extreme consequences from this basic familiarity or empathy; he only calls it, *egeo*, a 'desire.' Meister Eckhart, on the other hand, will rely on this notion of connaturality to say that 'in the ground' (= *esse*) of ourselves we know all things and we know God as perfectly as he knows us.

2. The ontological difference between connaturality and conformity

Connatural knowledge is that knowledge in which things show themselves by themselves—without abstractive activity on our behalf—as simply actual.[38] They can show themselves that way because being-real is the common 'perfection' that belongs to them and man. Such manifestation of reality occurs prior to any distinction between subject and object. One could say—but that is not Aquinas' vocabulary—that 'being-real,' actuality, is the 'horizon' within which the knower and the known meet. This horizon is not made by a human project; it is totally beyond anything categorial. Projecting, categorizing, abstracting, etc., are activities that produce knowledge of 'entia' [beings]; it is the milieu in which knower and known encounter each other, what they have in common, the 'esse' by which they are real. The horizon is not just any determination by which man and his world can come together, since it is the actuality of 'to-be'; it is their very core, or ground.

Reality so understood precedes the distinction between subject and object; it precedes therefore any effort to construe a bridge beyond that gap, be that bridge 'psychological,' epistemological or whatever. Knowledge by connaturality renders knowledge by conformity possible. Since this difference has appeared as one between *esse* and *ens*, between the ontological perfection of 'esse' and the ontic perfection of 'something,' it is properly an ontological difference. Connatural knowledge is the foundation of 'adequate' knowledge.

Objective knowledge—or representational thinking—renders *a* being present to itself and thus introduces otherness between knower and known. But it was the decisive discovery of Aristotle, although confined to a theory of knowledge and not expanded into one of ontology, that "the knower and the known are one." Cf. Thomas, quoting from *De Anima* III, 2; 426 a 16: "The sensible in act is the sense in act, and the intelligible in act is the intellect in act" (Ia 14, 2; Pegis p. 129). Although Thomas says of that quote ("in his quae sunt sine materia, idem est intellectus et quod intelligitur" [in those things that are without matter, the intellect and what it understands are the same]) that "it is universally true in all respects" (Ia 87, 1, ad 3; Pegis p. 428 mistranslated), he does not draw the consequence that Meister Eckhart will draw: through the connaturality we are 'actually' one with God.

Nevertheless, Aquinas insists on the ontological dimension of connaturality, and he sees that otherness—the subject-object distinction—is derivative with regard to the basic 'common nature' which is the rootedness in 'esse.' He says, for instance, that 'esse' is the *constitutivum formale* [formal constituent] both of man and of things, both of knower and of known. It is clear that in such a context it simply makes no sense to isolate a philosophical discipline called 'theory of knowledge': problems of knowledge can only be understood and solved from a preliminary inquiry into problems of being. It then appears that 'objective knowledge,' which produces true propositions, considers beings as something already there, already entering our horizon. In connatural knowledge, on the other hand, man encounters things without thematizing their otherness; there is no exteriority known in that kind of knowledge.

A word about Aquinas' usage of 'object' and 'subject.' 'Subject' translates for him 'hypokeimenon' [underlying thing]. It is what endures at the bottom in a threefold sense: 'suppositum' [supposit] or 'substantia' [substance] of accidents; the 'subject' in a proposition; the 'subject-matter' of a discipline (cf. the quote from Aristotle in Ia, 1, 3, obj. 1[39]). The word 'subject' thus by no means has the same signification as today—it is rather what we would call 'object' or 'objectivity.' The medieval term 'obiectum' designates in Thomas Aquinas the terminus of any kind of activity:

> Every act is either of an active power or of a passive power. Now, the object is to the act of a passive power as the principle and moving cause [obiectum comparatur ad actum potentiae passivae sicut principium et causa movens]. For colour is the principle of vision, inasmuch as it moves our sight. On the other hand, to the act of an active power the object is a term and end [ad actum autem potentiae activae comparatur obiectum ut terminus et finis]; just as the object of the power of growth is perfect quantity, which is the end of growth. (Ia 77, 3; Pegis p. 317)

It is clear that 'obiectum' here designates the Aristotelian 'entelecheia.' In the domain of the philosophy of knowledge: the 'end' or terminus is called the 'object of knowledge,' where we would rather say the 'subject matter.' E.g.: "In operations which pass to an external effect the object of the operation, which is taken as the term, exists outside the operator; in operations that remain in the operator [reflection, R.S.], the object signified as the term of operation resides in the operator" (Ia 14, 2; Pegis p. 129).

You see that Aquinas' understanding of the essence of knowledge tries to hold the middle between mere subjectivism (the object of knowledge is merely the result of a mental activity) and mere objectivism (the object of knowledge is an existing universal).[40] Aquinas says: knowledge has its foundation in the senses by which we counter the 'entia' [beings] around us ... and which mediate between the powers of the mind and the things: "Cognitio est media inter cognoscentem et obiectum" [Knowledge is an intermediary between the knower and the object] (De Ver. 2, 5, obj. 15).[41] But this middle-line is fully understood only if it is traced back to the ontological difference between 'esse' and 'ens.'

Indeed, Aquinas says that the knower and known become 'alike' in ontic knowledge: "Assimilatio cognoscentis ad cognitum" [assimilation of the knower and the known] (Contra Gentiles I, 65), or "similitudinem cogniti in cognoscente" [likeness of the thing known in the knower] (Contra Gentiles II, 77, 2).[42] Of course, the Aristotelian background of these formulations indicates that it is the form that occupies the middle position: the form 'in re' is the same as the form 'in mente'; thus the mind assimilates itself in appropriating the form of the thing known. Nevertheless, the condition that allows for such appropriation of form is a more basic kinship: namely that both the knower and the known partake in actuality. Only on that ground can the secondary act of one—Heisenberg's uncertainty principle—become the act of another: my studying it. The much-praised mediation, in Aquinas, between universalism and nominalism has its ground in his ontology of actuality. Only when that is seen can one understand the full scope of what is meant by the double determination of knowledge: determination by the subject (*cognitio secundum modum cognoscentis* [knowledge according to the mode of the knower]; *I Sent.* 38, 1, 2) and determination by the object (*esse tale* [to be such]). Likewise the duplicity, so required in the intellect, can only be grasped on that ground: duplicity of the active intellect (determining its knowledge) and the passive intellect (letting itself be determined). Finally, the very notion of 'conformity' shows that a middle domain is required: Aquinas' theory is not one of mental reproduction, but the thing is rendered conform to the mind (its material component is discarded), and the mind, conform to the thing (whose formal component modifies the mind).

The grounding of ontic knowledge in ontological knowledge— or of conformity in connaturality—appears finally in the theory of reflection: the knower knows himself in knowing the thing known. There is no place (at least at first sight) for non-objective self-knowledge in Aquinas, of the kind of the soul's knowledge by itself (Augustine). Reflection, in Aquinas, is always concomitant with empirical knowledge. Knowledge is self-knowledge of a knowing subject. Thus the subject-object distinction is further reduced: "idem est intellectus et quod intelligitur" [the intellect and what it understands are the same] (Ia 87, 1, ad 3; Pegis p. 428).

Such an identity of subject and object in knowledge is possible only by connatural knowledge—it *is* connatural knowledge (Rahner: *beim anderen sein* = *bei sich sein* [being with the other = being with oneself][43]): the subject appears as not yet distinguished from the object; the object is not yet another. "Since the intellect reflects upon itself, by such reflection it understands both its own act of understanding and the species by which it understands" (Ia 85, 2; Pegis p. 407). By the species—image drawn from the object—the intellect forms the concept of a thing; at the same time and by the same act the intellect knows its own act of intellection. Knowing a thing and knowing itself is possible for the mind only if thing and self are of the same nature, are connatural.

Reflection thus is not an additional activity; it is a dimension of every and any act of knowing—that dimension by which connaturality appears most clearly.[44] "Manifestum est quod [intellectus, R.S.] ex eo quod cognoscit intelligibile, intelligit ipsum suum intelligere" [It is manifest that by knowing the intelligible object [the intellect] understands also its own act of understanding] (Ia 14, 2, ad 3; Pegis p. 131). Thus knowledge is always 'more' than the cognition of this or that thing. One could say that this 'more' corresponds to the excess of actuality over the actual thing.

3. The scope of connatural knowledge

If connaturality is based on actuality, it must encompass the entire human being. And indeed, according to Aquinas, 'connaturality' designates a kinship with all other things that goes beyond cognition: in the moral treatises IaIIae and IIaIIae, 'connaturality' is a key term that designates a grasp of what we would perhaps call values (moral entities) whose truth is not guaranteed rationally but through "good disposition" (*virtus cognoscitiva bene disposita... Bona dispositione appetitivae virtutis* [the knowing power is well disposed... Good disposition of the appetitive power]; IIaIIae 51, 3, ad 1).[45]

To illustrate this point, it is clear that Scheler's notion of correlation between values and levels of the human subject derives from this theory of connaturality—or rather, both derive from Plotinus, *Enneads* I, 6, 9 (*Wär nicht Dein Auge sonnenhaft* [If your eye were not like the sun] ...).[46] In Aquinas it is the moral dispositions of the knower that serve as paradigms for connatural knowledge: the just man, without reasoning, knows immediately what a just act is and is able to distinguish it from an unjust one. Justice = "dispositio iudicantis, ex qua habet idoneitatem ad recte iudicandum" [the disposition of the one who judges, from which he has the aptitude for judging rightly] (IIaIIae 60, 1, ad 1). Judgement is here called "iudicare per modum inclinationis" [to judge by inclination] (Ia 1, 6, ad 3; Pegis p. 11; i.e., *habitus*). Knowledge through connaturality seizes many things that remain excluded from discursive and rational knowledge. Connaturality can be explained as a receptive union with the goodness of things: an "affective or experiential knowledge [*cognitio affectiva vel experimentalis*] by which one experiences within oneself the taste for divine sweetness and the enjoyment of the divine will" (IIaIIae 97, 2, ad 2).

It is necessary to see that this complementary type of knowledge reveals, in Thomas' eyes, only the basic elements of knowledge in general: a belonging-together in the same 'nature,' in the same actuality. Thus what is primarily grasped in connatural knowledge is the individual reality of a thing—hence the metaphoric language where knowledge of the individual cannot be expressed rationally. This doctrine is derived from Pseudo Dionysius' teaching of world-harmony.

In the noetic act, then, connaturality appears as a dynamism: an inclination (not just any one) that carries us toward anything that actually exists.[47] Connaturality designates the desire for an ever closer contact with reality, with sheer actuality. What carries the human mind towards the knowledge of essences is a more radical parenthood with everything real. Connaturality is not the will; this has sometimes been a source of confusion: Aquinas, indeed, speaks of a 'natural desire' for actuality. Rather, both will and intellect are forms of connaturality. They are connatural acts. Our habitual dispositions show only how we possess in advance what we want to know or what we will: they are particular cases of the ontological inclination towards everything actual.

Summary: Connatural knowledge[48]

— relates to rational knowledge as *esse* [being] to *ens* [beings];
— includes all faculties of the human subject—intellectual, volitional, affective—and is their root;
— brings the human 'nature' with all its general and individual perfections into the act of knowing;

— differs from cognition (by sense or intellect) as actuality from
potency: "The sensible in act is the sense in act, and the intelligible in act is the intellect in act... [I]t follows that sense or
intellect is distinct from the sensible or intelligible object only
insofar as both are in potentiality" (Ia 14, 2; Pegis p. 129).

Connatural knowledge means that what is 'intelligible in potency'
has already somehow shown itself; has already appeared to us in
a 'precursory appearance.' Connatural knowledge actually knows
what is potentially knowable—it is driven towards its actuality,
and it seeks to wrest its essence from it, to negate its potentiality.
Connatural knowledge is the anticipatory familiarity with 'esse.' By
connatural knowledge we belong to all things, and all things to us.

What in modernity is called 'object,' for Aquinas is the "ens extra
animam" [the being outside the soul], precisely that aspect which is
not the being-aspect ('esse') of things.[49] And what we call 'subject'
he would call the 'intellectus possibilis' [possible intellect], precisely
that aspect of the mind that is not actual. The subject is the subject of 'possible knowledge.' But such an object is not real—strictly
speaking. A thing outside the mind exists only in our representation,
namely insofar as a real being, an actual being, is thought not in its
actuality but as potential, as 'intelligibile in potentia' [potentially
intelligible]. Actuality is precisely what is irreducible to 'intelligibile
in potentia.' Likewise the subject as the subject of possible knowledge is nothing actual; it exists only in representation. Connatural
knowledge chases everything potential; it precedes it.

For Aquinas, the relation between subject and object (in the modern sense) is simply a representation: "Action that remains in the
agent [*actio quae manet in agente*] does not really mediate between
the agent and the object [*non est realiter medium inter agens et
obiectum*], but only intentionally [*secundum modum significandi*]"
(Ia 54, 1, ad 3; not in Pegis). The subject-object relation is here said
to be merely immanent; it does not step beyond the mind of the
knower; it is not transcending the knower.

To express the same matter from the point of view of truth: the
truth that is obtained by conforming the subject's affirmations to
the object's perfections is derivative; there is a more fundamental
truth that Aquinas' ontology of *esse* points to: the truth established

by the knowledge that is really transcending the knower, and which is given with his actuality, his *esse*.

Thus, prior to the substantial otherness, prior to the split between subjective and objective 'ens,' Aquinas thinks of an identity of things in their act-to-be. A relation of otherness, of objectivity, can only be *thought*. The truth that occurs primarily in the knowledge of things is their auto-manifestation in as much as they are actual. This results from the constitution of a notion of actuality which, contrary to Aristotle, has no corresponding potentiality. What is primarily true, in this perspective, is not the 'ens' (individual, definable), but the 'esse,' reality itself. Not beings, but being. Only on the ground of such ontological truth can ontic truth be true. But such ontological truth has nothing to do with the concept. Only ontic truth has. And only ontic truth presupposes a distance between knower and known.

I already quoted the text Ia 16, 2 in which Aquinas opposed the 'veritas rerum' [truth of things] to the definition of truth by "conformitas intellectus et rei" [conformity of intellect and thing]. The 'veritas rerum' is defined by the thing possessing its own form. So, we can again draw on the double function of the form to understand this duplicity of knowledge: the form, in as much as it "dat esse" [gives being], makes the thing ontologically true; the form, in as much as it determines the thing's essence, makes it ontically true. Likewise, the mind grasps its own ontological truth in reflecting upon itself—all the while knowing a thing (reflection is always concomitant with cognition): "secundum hoc cognoscit veritatem intellectus quod super se ipsum reflectitur" [consequently, it is because the intellect reflects upon itself that it knows truth] (*De Ver.* 1, 9).

One could call connatural truth 'evidence.'

I recommend that on this entire matter you read questions 84–87; Pegis pp. 376–428.

4. Connatural knowledge and the active intellect

The key problem now becomes: what consequences does connatural knowledge entail for the constitution of the human mind? How are we to understand the mind if prior to the effort of joining essences to concepts in a proposition, truth is to be understood as transcendence? As the mind's stepping beyond itself towards what is real, around it?

I translate a text from Aquinas' Commentary on Aristotle's *De Anima*.[50] First Aristotle's own text:

> Since in every class of things, as in nature as a whole, we find two factors involved, (1) a matter which is potentially all the particulars included in the class, (2) a cause which is productive in the sense that it makes them all (the latter standing to the former as, for instance, an art to its material), these distinct elements must likewise be found within the soul. And in fact mind is what it is by virtue of becoming all things, while there is another which is what it is by virtue of making all things. This is a sort of positive state like light; for in a sense light makes potential colours into actual colours. Mind in this sense of it is separable, impassible, unmixed, since it is in its essential nature activity... This alone is immortal and eternal, and without it nothing thinks." (*De. An.* III, 5; 430 a 10–25)[51]

Now Aquinas' commentary:

> In its intellective part, the mind is sometimes in potency, sometimes in actuality. It is thus necessary that there be these differences in the intellective soul: on the one hand, the intellect, by which all things can become intelligible, and this is the passive intellect ... on the other hand, the intellect that actually turns all things into things actually intelligible [*actu intelligibilia*]; this is called *intellectus agens*, and it is somewhat like a habit." (*In III De An.*, l. 10; n. 728)

We already heard that connatural knowledge expressed itself in the 'habits,' the correct natural dispositions. Now one of these 'habits' is said to be our disposition to make things actually knowable. The active intellect acts "somewhat like a habit" only because, like a habit, it is always actually there, inclining us towards things. The point of the text is: the part of the mind that is "sometimes in potency, sometimes in actuality" refers to objective knowledge. It is with regard to a given thing that the mind may be first potentially knowing, then actually knowing (that is what should happen in a lecture: first you know about Aquinas' theory of knowledge potentially, and when you walk out of here, you know of it in full actuality).

Knowledge by conformity occurs 'sometimes'; hence its actuality is 'actualitas per accidens' [accidental actuality]. Knowledge by connaturality occurs in the nature of the mind; in Aristotle's words, unmixed, immortal, eternal. The mind actively transcends itself always; transcendence is its nature, its disposition. This or that object can be known only because the mind *is* nothing other than actual transcendence.

From what was said of the scope of connatural knowledge, it is clear that the active mind is not merely 'mental.' Rather the actuality that precedes this or that objective knowledge encompasses the entirety of individual and general perfections—in the language of human faculties, it encompasses sensibility. You remember the frequent quote from the *De Anima*, according to which the intellect in act and the intelligible in act, the sense in act and the sensible in act, are one. Thus sensibility and intelligence are the two branches of human knowledge.

The activity of knowing, in so far as it involves the entire human being, is called connatural knowledge; in so far as it is an activity that never ceases, it is called active intellect.

'Intelligere' must be understood in a very broad sense here; as 'understanding,' perhaps. Sensibility as well as will are drawn into that activity. The possible intellect corresponds to 'ens' and to conformity; the active intellect, to 'esse' and connaturality. "The human mind is divided into actuality and potentiality only accidentally [*intelligens non se habet ut agens et patiens, nisi per accidens*]; indeed, for an intelligible thing to be united to the intellect, both action and passion are required. But what understanding is in itself results from such junction of activity and potency" (*De Ver.* 8, 6). To obtain adequate propositions, we have to actualize potencies in the mind. But such junction only shows what knowledge is in itself: sheer actuality. Actuality is thus the principle of 'potential' knowledge.

The theory of the active intellect[52] is at the core of three other philosophical problematics in Thomas Aquinas: 1. The active intellect makes sensible things intelligible by 'abstracting' from them; 2. The active intellect superelevates the sensible within the intelligible by 'illuminating phantasms' (cf. Rahner[53]); 3. The active intellect 'illumines' by exhibiting the difference between 'esse' and 'ens' in things sensible, i.e., by placing things sensible under the 'first principles.'

Abstraction, knowledge by representation, first principles, all originate in the active intellect. This is not the place to develop these elements. But they form an excellent transition to the conceptualism of William of Ockham.

III.

William of Ockham's Conceptualism

Preliminary remarks.

Late Scholasticism is often viewed as having produced little original thought: as if the fourteenth and fifteenth centuries had refined what had been worked out earlier—but refined to the degree of absurdity in detail and mere verbosity. This view is correct for many figures of that period, but utterly false for Ockham, Eckhart, Cusa. However, this atmosphere of disputation over marginal details in a constituted body of doctrine allows one to understand some aspects in the writings of all three of these. In fact, with all three the—or 'a'—decisive reversal is taken towards modernity. Ockham will leave his shadow over the place where he studied and taught—Oxford—until today, with the rejection of metaphysical assumptions of any type of realism of universals, and his effort to base philosophy on radical empiricism. Eckhart will have a descendancy to some extent in Luther, but massively in so-called German Idealism and, in a way, in Heidegger. Nicholaus Cusanus has his disciples in Italy (Ficinus, Pico della Mirandola, Giordano Bruno) and in Germany (Leibniz at least).

William of Ockham: [born] 1285 near London, enters the Franciscan Order; studies, of course, Duns Scotus; teaches and writes, of course, a Commentary on the *Sentences* by Peter Lombard; becomes accused—also naturally!—of teaching unecclesiastical doctrines; flees to Bavaria, where he spends twenty years and dies in Munich 1349.[54] In fact he takes up the defense of the Bavarian king whose claim as emperor is challenged. He is said to have told him: "Emperor, defend me with your sword and I shall defend you with my pen."[55]

1. Experience and universals

I take up three points mentioned at the end of what I said about the active intellect in Aquinas in order to show the radical negation of connaturality in Ockham.

a. Abstraction.[56] To abstract an intelligible element from a sensible thing is to place the efficient causality of knowledge in our mind. That is why Aquinas (after Aristotle) precisely spoke of the active intellect: it is our mental activity that 'renders' all things knowable. In such a perspective, experience is only the material cause in knowledge; the form is the 'formal' cause, and the concept the final cause. With the formal and the final causes there is a universal given that we can systematize according to genus and species. I refer you back to Aristotle's *De Anima* on this theory of abstraction. Without a specific form that exists, individualized, in a thing, i.e., without a universal that somehow transcends the momentary experience, there is no knowledge for an Aristotelian.

For Ockham, now, sense experience becomes the genuine efficient cause of knowledge. That sounds very innocent; but he holds that we do not need anything more than to look with our senses at the things given in the world, or to look with our inner eye at the states or acts of our mind in order to have the origin of knowledge. Abstraction still applies, but it is totally transformed with regard to the Aristotelian tradition: abstraction is the constitution of a concept but which has no root in the thing. As he says in the *Quodlibets*: "The abstractive cognition which is simple and comes first in order of origination is not proper to a singular thing, but a cognition common to many" (Boehner p. 32).[57] But how is this explained? "We have no proper and simple cognition of a singular thing, as long as we can get no specific knowledge of it."[58] And now the dismantling of the Aristotelian understanding of experience. "[F]or instance, when somebody, approaching from a distance, causes in me a sense-perception with the help of which I can judge only that what I see is an existent." Experience is the experience of an 'ens' [a being], as Thomas would call it; "it is the cognition of an existent, and of nothing more general," Ockham says. In Aquinas abstraction had the role (and possibility) of drawing a universal element, called essence, form, or nature, out of the *ens*. This possibility is what Ockham dismisses. The direct experience of individual things and particular events is deprived of its ground for unification into a concept that would apply to many such instances. Rather the concept is what we inject—fictionalizing, he says in his commentary on Peter Lombard's *Sentences*:[59] "The universal is not generated [vs. Duns Scotus, R.S.] but it comes about through abstraction, which is nothing less than a certain fiction" (*I Sent.* d. 2, q. 8 E). So, this is the first point: the transformation of abstraction into fiction, or injection of a concept that has no root in anything universal given with experience. As our text says: "Concerning the instance of a man coming from a distance, I say that I judge him to be a living being, since I am already in the possession of the concept 'living being' (animal), a concept that is a genus... If I did not already possess the concept of the genus 'animal,' I would judge only that this which is seen is something" (Boehner p. 35). The thing thus prompts the injection of a concept—without mediation coming from the thing: "We always get an impression of the concept 'ens,' because if the object is sufficiently close, a concept of the species and the concept 'ens' are simultaneously caused by the extra-mental singular thing" (ibid.). What is the ground for such rejection of continuity between individual experience and the—fictitious—conceptualizing of the mind?

b. 'Phantasms.' Aristotelian empiricism means that to obtain a concept we have to rely on a representation, an image, a phantasm coming from the thing and carrying the formal universal. What breaks down in Ockham's account is the pivotal, mediating role of the phantasm or 'species.' The concept of experience in Ockham is such that it cannot originate a phantasm. "An active and a passive element, that is, object and knowledge—both united, and the result is there without further mediation" (*II Sent.* q. 15 O; not in Boehner). The active intellect would indeed be necessary only if it had the material of phantasms, of representations, to act upon, and if it were considered able to extract intelligibles from them. You have to see that Ockham's refusal of common natures to things hinges on this rejection of the images in knowing, which entails, on the side of the knower, the rejection of active intellect. Because of this breakdown of image-mediation, the universal concept is only a thought-thing; it is no ontological determination of the 'ens.' The universal, he says, "is only in the mind and hence not in the thing" (*I Sent.* d. 2., q. 7 G). In fact, he turns the polemic around and says against Aquinas: "Nothing outside the mind is predicated of many things, except by convention" (Boehner p. 13). So, the same thing is not—as the Aristotelians hold—individual and universal at the same time, but from different points of view; a thing is merely individual, and what is universal has no 'fundamentum in re' [foundation in the thing]. The entire effort to think the individualization of an essence or nature in a form is thus eliminated from the field of philosophizing together with the middle term between universal and singular, the 'phantasm.'

c. Principles. The question then arises of how our principles of injecting concepts come about. This is the crucial question once the active intellect cannot be considered the abstractive force any longer. Instead of principles of universalization of a thing known, Ockham speaks of 'signs' that are in the mind. In Aristotelianism, that which, when apprehended, makes us know something else, is the concept derived from the intuited form. Now Ockham: "[A sign] is that which, when apprehended, makes us know something else" (Boehner p. 53). The 'sign' par excellence is a word; how? In as much as it is caused by the sense experience. "Any effect is a sign." "And in this way also a barrel-hoop signifies the wine in the inn" (ibid.). In the narrower sense, however, this text pursues, a sign "stands in for something else." And "in this sense, a word is not a natural sign of anything." Why? Because in Ockham's view there is between the word and the thing it signifies no relation that is comparable to the barrel-hoop (or the yellow shell indicating gasoline) and the wine in the inn. There is no continuity between signifier and signified; only convention.

Thus there is no use indeed for 'principles' that would regulate abstraction and the obtention of a concept. A sign is simply a direction indicated by the mind, an 'intentio.' But 'intention' here means 'institution' or convention: "tantum ex institutione" [only from convention] (*I Sent.* d. 2, q. 8 E). A sign is "quoddam fictum," something invented. It is the utter sound by which we call upon what we signify: "Non plus quam vox est sui significati" [No more than the sound belongs to what it signifies] (*I Sent.* d. 2, q. 7 T). This replacement of principles of the active intellect by signs of convention leads to the impossibility, of course, of what previous philosophers called knowledge. There is no knowledge possible, for Ockham, if knowledge means to look somehow into the inner makeup, the inner constitution of things. This gaze into the 'natura intrinseca' [intrinsic nature] is possible only for God, he says. Man, on the contrary, does not have more than signs to point to this or that which he encounters. No active intellect can produce in our minds the natural whatness of a thing.

The metaphysical transcendence, the stepping beyond the mind to encounter the real whatness of things, is rendered impossible by Ockham's replacing intellectual principles with signs. From what I said earlier about Peter Abelard, you see that Abelard's intuitions now come again to the fore, after a massive predominance of Aristotelian trust in the continuity between knower and thing known.

2. Against connaturality

Ontologically, Ockham's position forces him, of course, to reject the analogy of being derived from the preeminence of 'esse' [being, to be]. The point is that his ontology by no means allows for the recognition of something like the act-to-be as ground for connaturality. Since the common imbeddedness of subject and object is now torn apart, the notion of being is equivocal (Boehner p. 102). Consequence: I only know what is individual. At times Ockham even states that one cannot speak of both Socrates and any other human being univocally as 'man.' Rather than saying 'Socrates is a human being' one should say "Socrates is Socrates" (*I Sent.* d. 2, q. 7 X)—the two propositions mean exactly the same thing!

Universality, in Aquinas, was the property of the act-to-be. Grounded on that act, universality was also attributable to species and genera. Now, universality pertains exclusively to signs. The problem of universals is taken out of the realm of metaphysics and confined to that of language. This is, of course, music to an Anglo-American philosophical mind up to the present day—although

Ockham still retained, at least in some texts, it seems, the universality of substance. But how is this grounded? What distinguishes
Ockham from his contemporary English disciples is the trust in
God's governance. Quite as later in Luther, there is a kind of *Allein-
wirksamkeit Gottes* [sole efficacy of God] which holds the universe
together. And the world is held together, not by God's granting
esse, but by God's will: things have nothing to do with one another;
there is no real communication between them, but by a constant
influx of God's will, they remain substances.

This is very peculiar to any Aristotelian mind: ontology is now
dependent on two other disciplines which earlier it used to found,
namely logic and morality (as doctrine of the will). There is no 'rela-
tio realis' between things, and not even between God and things.
This 'real relation' was, as I have explained it in the two contexts of
ontology and the philosophy of knowledge, the very core of Aquinas' philosophizing: in ontology, due to the communication of act,
and in knowledge, due to connaturality. Here, knowledge becomes
governed by logic, and hence principles turn into 'signs' in language; and ontology is ultimately rooted in a philosophy of will;
hence the coherence of the universe is now exclusively a matter
of divine benevolence—cosmology is theological, not philosophical.[60] In this respect Ockham proves to be genuinely Franciscan, in
that—quite as Scotus earlier—he does not care to draw the line as
clearly as Aquinas did between what the 'lumen naturale' [natural
light] can know and what requires revelation in order to be known.

Ockham's universe is derationalized, individualized, and without
an immanent contexture of being. It is a complex of singulars,[61]
which repeat the same features—primarily substance—but such
features may vanish tomorrow, since they depend on the 'potentia Dei absoluta' [absolute power of God]. We know these many
individual things by immediate evidence, not by abstraction in the
classical sense. At the same time, this elimination of an a priori
construction of ontological features also opens the way to a further
step in the recognition of the autonomy of things, a further step in
the direction of autonomous science.

The gist of Ockham's attack on the idea of connaturality should
be seen clearly.[62] Schematically put, Western philosophy inherits
from the Greeks the representation of nature as an eternal order,

subsisting in and by itself. And it inherits from Judaism the representation of a world that is made. Much of the medieval speculative effort can be explained by the consequences from this double origin. One consequence: How is the idea of making to be reconciled with that of nature as an eternal whole, self-subsisting, self-sustaining? Another consequence: How is it possible for man to properly know nature, if by knowing we mean not only receiving, but, as Aquinas did, a reciprocity of determination based on a basic actuality or activity (active intellect)?

The solution to these problems given by Aquinas and others was to say: God's making, creation, is itself rational. The rational order of the universe does not contradict the dogma of creation; rather it tells us something about what God is himself: truth, beauty, etc.... The solution given by Ockham is quite different; it is basically religious, too—despite the appearance. Ockham says: God, as absolutely autonomous and free cause, has made the world the way it is, but with no essential link to rationality. The world appears, then, to Ockham no longer as a 'kosmos' (necklace), but as utterly contingent, irreducible to reason. The step from 'esse' (as ontological concept) to 'intellectus agens' [active intellect] (a concept of knowledge) showed precisely, in Aquinas, the trust in the basic rationality of being. That being is not only intelligible, but *as* intelligible, ordered. With Ockham, it is the unity of 'on' [being] and 'logos' [reason] that disappears from thinking. Rational ontology is no longer held to be possible—a totally new way of looking at the world.

The consequence is that knowledge becomes deprived of its foundation. And Ockham is one of the forerunners of modernity in as much as he clearly acknowledges this missing ground, and furthermore, in as much as 'method' now replaces, or begins to replace, ontology. But you have to see the three steps in the rise of modernity as prefigured here by Ockham: the Greek-Biblical junction of rational order and creation; the unity of being and knowing as founded by that junction (unity expressed by 'esse' and 'connaturality'); the collapse of the trust in rational order and the return of the trust in God's making, now deprived of its link to the Greek representations.

3. Conceptualism and necessity

What has been called Ockham's 'nominalism' should rather be called 'conceptualism': the universals exist in concepts only; it is true, though, as I stated, that he sometimes goes further and says that universals are only words. Let me trace this conceptualism to the so-called Franciscan school.[63] Duns Scotus had taught that contingent effects can only derive from contingent causes. Consequences from thinking, hence also from God understood as rational being, can only lead to necessary consequences. Now, the contingency in the world is undeniable; hence the cause of the world cannot be a rational God, or God 'qua' *ratio*, but rather God's will. In the ultimate ground, as Scotus called it, God is something alien to reason. The radical cause of all events is a moment in God that operates contingently—his will, which is not determined rationally.

Ockham takes this framework a step further. Indeed, the very reasoning by which Scotus steps from the contingency in the world to a contingency in God already arouses Ockham's suspicion. "Nec credo quod per rationem posset hoc probari, quod prima causa contingenter causat" [Nor do I believe that this can be proven by reason, that the first cause causes contingently] (*I Sent.*, d. 35, q. 2 C). Thus there is doubt in Ockham even about the transition from the second causes' contingency to the first cause, altogether. Thus not only rational operation is unprovable in God (as it was for Scotus— with the result of his insistence on God's love, and a return from metaphysics to faith), but any efficacy in God is totally unprovable. Such is the consequence of the disruption of the philosophy of knowledge from ontology. Once anything universal—not only Platonic ideas, but even such a tenuous universal as the always-individual *actus essendi* [act of being]—is broken down, there is no ground to prove any knowledge at all to be correct. Ockham has seen this; hence his decided turn towards empiricism and method. As universal (and that is why he should be called a conceptualist, not a nominalist) he only retains the principle of non-contradiction.

Universal contingency, in Ockham, derives ultimately from a principle of faith; he would quote again and again the first sentence of the Christian creed: "I believe in the omnipotent Father." Thus he opposes rational or logical necessity and universal contingency—but on grounds of belief. That is, of course, quite coherent, since it would assuredly be absurd to rationally argue for the absence of rationality in the universe.

So, despite his conceptualism, he maintains a ground for thought that links the Creator and the created, namely faith; but with this ground we lose sight of what is properly philosophical in the Middle Ages. However, Ockham also retains a second ground for discourse and, in fact, for science: the principle of non-contradiction. These two grounds are all that remain of the old 'universals.' And you have to see that these hypostatized universals collapsed already with Aquinas' reduction of perfections to 'esse.'

But what is the scope of application of the principle of non-contradiction? "Non includit contradictionem deum assumere naturam asininam" [It is not contradictory for God to take on the nature of an ass] (Centiloqu. concl. 6 A). Ockham uses the principles of non-contradiction primarily in a negative sense, and restricts its scope of application quite considerably, to say the least. For instance, God cannot make that things past have not happened—here is a positive[64] instance of the principle of non-contradiction. But it is well possible for him "quod ignis de potentia Dei absoluta potest recipere frigiditatem" [that, by the absolute power of God, fire is able to receive cold] (I Sent., d. 1, q. 3 S). One is left with the impression, then, that Ockham attempts to restrict the scope of application of the principle of non-contradiction, all the while operating with the conviction that both in scientific and in theological matters this principle somehow does apply. There is an evident conflict in his writings between the application of that principle and the validity, said to be universal, of the principle of divine omnipotence.

Ockham's picture of the world thus appears under these traits: out of his 'potentia absoluta' [absolute power] God has created the given world-order—not rationally, but from an impulse of his will. This world order can, at any time, be abolished or totally transformed by another such act of God. In that sense, the universe as a whole, as well as in its parts, is thoroughly contingent. And that is the reason why a rational grasp of the universe, why any realism of universals, is impossible. All necessities that seem to obtain within the world are simple effects of God's will, but they are not logical, absolute. The cause for such apparent necessities is not a rational principle, but God's given ordinance. Ockham's conceptualism thus results from his reinterpretation of the relation between contingent and necessary truths. There are no necessary truths per se; only truths that seem to us to be necessary because they derive from a given will-disposition of the omnipotent cause. One could even say that the principle of divine omnipotence is the unknown X in all statements about the world, in all cognition. Because of this unknown X, cognition is never sure; concepts, although they contain universal elements, are never protected from doubt. At any one moment new facts may arise that entail the modification of a given law of motion and even the modification of entire scientific theories.

What appears quite beautifully in Ockham—and what modernity will develop much further, of course—is the link between method and a kind of anxiety, called 'doubt' in Descartes... One could say that Ockham's way of understanding contingency and necessity eliminates anything conceivable from the things around us. This could be shown, for instance, by tracing his notion of 'form': it is much narrower in scope than in Aquinas or even Aristotle. The substantial form is now deprived of anything universal; and together with its universality, the individual form loses its rational character. It cannot be theoretically grasped; but this presence of the universal in the particular was precisely the decisive element in the old theory of forms. In Ockham, both form and matter become utterly singular.[65]

Knowledge, then, becomes purely intuitive. I have said that there is no abstractive bridge any longer in Ockham, which leads from the thing to a concept. We now see the reason why. No bridge, but a leap—a leap over representation, phantasms, images. And the title for this leap is 'cognitio intuitiva' [intuitive knowledge]. The concept is generated by the mind, and only 'prompted' by sense experience. More precisely, the act of knowing is in fact double, in Ockham: besides immediate sense-experience there is, equally immediate, intellectual intuition. He needs this second act in order to account for concepts altogether. The first act is called 'cognitio experimentalis' [experiential knowledge]. Once this intellectual intuition is eliminated from philosophy—and it appears already here how much of a leftover it is—the time will have come for Descartes.

4. Absolute power and contradiction

I have explained why Ockham's elimination of universals and his exaltation of singulars should go under the title of 'conceptualism' rather than 'nominalism.' What is as stake is the locus, as well as the nature, of the successor to the universals. Ockham: that locus remains the concept, not the mere name; but its nature changes as the concept turns into a 'fact,' i.e., a *factum*, something made by our reason. I have shown why the sole knowledge of the world that remains possible is bound to be intuitive knowledge, and that—despite his use of the classical term *forma*—singulars no longer are considered to possess any complexity, any thickness, any formal wealth such that a universal could be drawn from their form. A universal essence would limit God's omnipotence, since he would have to stick to a model: four limbs, one torso, and one head to any human being.

For the generation and corruption of the singular, this implies—one further step on the road to modernity—that things can no longer be viewed as growing according to their common nature.[66] Rather each singular is *made*, without such ontological moorings as essences used to provide. The maker, whether human or divine, does not follow a naturally given form; rather he arranges and rearranges freely material parts. This means that singulars do not appear according to a pattern one can know in advance: something like Goethe's 'originary plant'; but if there are affinities among things, these too are *contingent*. They depend solely on the pure effectiveness without rules, working on an infinity of possibles—God's will. In Aristotelian terms, *technē* [art] has eclipsed *physis* [nature]. There is no way of maintaining the separation between two realms of phenomena, one growing by itself, the other made. Everything is individually made by God's 'relative' power. And much more could be made by his 'absolute' power.

This is doubtless the chief instance of Ockham's axiom of parsimony, namely to explain the world with recourse to the fewest principles possible (what Jean Buridan later labeled 'Ockham's razor'). The itinerary of so-called nominalism was to be traced by that axiom: the goal was to reduce further and further the elements needed to reach an understanding of the world. Thus Ockham at times reduced all Aristotelian causes to one: efficient cause. Buridan himself occupied a moderate position in this struggle for intellectual poverty, and did not follow the trend to extremes such as the atomization of time and the ensuing atomization of causation. Once again, this trimming process inflicted on the body of metaphysics is possible only because of a strong faith in God's absolute power. This enables Ockham, among other things, to play out thought experiments.

I should like to show[67] how the sole principle of contradiction—to which, as I have said, Ockham reduces the traditional profusion of *archai kai aitiai* [principles and causes]—how this principle is a principle of power. Indeed he states: "Absolute power can make anything which does not imply a contradiction" (*Quodlibeta* VI, q. 1; ed. Wey, 1980, p. 586).[68]

This proposition is logical in that it introduces a formal criterion into the reality of power. But how so? An absolute power has to be, by definition, without limits—inner as well as outer limits. The point here is to understand that the principle of non-contradiction does not set any limit to God's absolute power. It would rather be limiting for any power to make *and* not to make at the same time and from the same point of view. Indeed, that conflict would militate against what he calls absoluteness or infinity. It would even destroy the very notion of power. Thus what is confining, for any power, is contradiction, not the necessity to follow non-contradiction. This necessity, on the contrary, makes it absolute power. It is the condition for its effectiveness.

The relation of power to contradiction as I quoted it from the *Quodlibeta* means: anything and everything that does not imply a thing's simultaneous being and non-being is possible. This possibility must be understood as real possibility, not only thinkability. It is the possibility for God to create different worlds. God's 'power,' in the Scholastics, always denotes God's effectiveness *ad extra*, on the created. In fact, that effectiveness as governed by absolute power leaves thinkability *by us* far behind.

First point to be retained about absolute power: the principle of non-contradiction does not limit it, but that principle describes its essence.

Second point: the exteriority of power. It does not take the place, in any sense, of something like Aquinas' 'connaturality.' It does not connect substances among themselves. Rather it disrupts any representation of the world as a continuous fabric. Singulars remain utterly foreign to each other, with no entitative bridge; and God's intervention upon them remains equally foreign, with no preexisting order of ideas making it understandable in advance.

Third point: the enfranchisement of singulars and the thesis of absolute power are mutually dependent. Test it by the change of one of the terms: if the singulars were connected to one another by something like connaturality, God's power would be finite: he would pre-figure that order of connaturality. Conversely, the independence of singulars would become unthinkable if God's power were not absolute, but if *potentia ordinata* [ordained power] were the last word about his power: then singulars would be exposed to no contingency, and their given order would be their essence.

Fourth and last point: the principle of non-contradiction is the logical core not only of God's absolute power, but also of everything's singularity in the world. Only God's absolute power can maintain singulars as fully identical with themselves. The principle of identity is thus derivative of the principle of non-contradiction which governs first of all God's omnipotence. Only once enfranchised can the singular equal itself, A = A, without also equaling its own universal essence or its own participated act-to-be.

5. Natural order dispersed

The medieval mind is altogether a mind obsessed with order. The feudal relations are relations of order, faith gives order to one's life, and all regional orders are justified by one grand order. For this, the various authors have different names: Augustine, as I said, called it 'eternal law'; others, 'nature'; others still 'participation'; etc. One can add that in all of these constructs the decisive ordering feature has been teleology. One could show in detail how Eternal law, Nature, Participation etc. stand or fall with the representation of a final cause toward which all things aim.

Now the points just mentioned about Ockham have a consequence that truly goes beyond the boundaries of medieval thought: singulars as separated from each other, as dependent solely on God's absolute power, as fully identical with themselves—constitute a *dispersed* world.

The opposite of dispersion so understood is teleology. Now I said that with his option—if that is the term—for the biblical God against the Greek ultimate representation of order, indeed his option for the God of the Old Testament, Ockham applies his razor to the set of causes as well. There is some hesitation about form and matter in his writings; when he comments on Aristotle's *Physics*, these are the two causes that he needs. In the *Summa Logicae*, the Sum of Logic, he holds that—as I have also said—efficient causality is all we need. Every additional cause or principle would enter into conflict with the tenet of *creatio ex nihilo* [creation from nothing]. Once again: the principle of non-contradiction does not inhibit that creation; rather absolute power realizes that principle. This principle states that a thing is nothing beside itself. It is justified, or at least instantiated, by the fact that God's power creates and annihilates, indeed, things independently from one another. The coming-into-being of the world and of every singular thing is 'out of nothingness'; so also the going-out-of-being is—not 'into nothingness' (that may be the case as well), but—out of nothingness: namely, not determined by chromosome fatigue, but by God's will.

This can be shown in many ways. In the *Summa Logicae*, he gives the example of separable and non-separable accidents: having red hair is an accident that is separable from my substance; having a head on my shoulders, not. Now Ockham: "The inseparable accident is the one that cannot be naturally taken away without altering the subject—although it can be so taken away by the divine power" (*Summa Logicae*, I, 25). This is to say that God's power could preserve me as a human subject, although beheaded. There goes the 'form' 'man' as the end possessed: as *entelecheia*. Ockham proposes many other arguments and examples, the point always remaining that God's absolute power has both an effect of preservation (*gubernatio mundi* [governance of the world]) and of dispersal ... not only *possible* dispersal, but the reduction of essences to singulars already disperses these.

The triad *potestas absoluta* [absolute power]–principle of non-contradiction–singularization suffices to dethrone teleology from the rank of ultimacy that it held since classical Greece. Therefore, in the series of concluding points I made last week, I presented Ockham not so much as the one who brings the medieval heritage to fulfillment, but rather who takes an incipient step out of it. The heart of that transgression is his contesting the ultimacy of natural ends. This is the most disruptive consequence of what I called the thinning out of experience: namely, that in encountering sensible substances, we no longer encounter a material thick enough to yield a universal—in this case, and always for the Medievals first and foremost, a universal end. That would suppose a 'real universal,' one that is at work in me and pulls the development of chromosomes to the shape made of four limbs, a torso and a head. If I can become a fully developed being without having my head, then discontinuity not only separates singulars from other singulars; it separates more harshly still every singular from itself. Not only is creation as a whole deprived of any unifying teleological focus; but every being in it is so deprived. "God is the immediate and sufficient cause of every effect" (*II Sent.*, q. 3). Thereby singularity, one can say, becomes absolutized.

6. Dispersion in God

But the metaphysician in us rebounds—like Rasputin, too tough to kill. If God is the immediate and sufficient cause of every effect, does this not establish between God and creature a strong ontological relation: of cause and effect, of continuous creation, of divine effective presence?

Not so. Communication is shut off in that direction as well—entitative, immediate communication. Indeed, immediate causation does not imply immediate presence for Ockham. I mentioned what for him replaces connatural communication: signs and their signification. I also mentioned the Christian appropriation of Greek paradigmatism: the 'divine ideas' that, from Augustine onward, are held to prefigure the world in God's intellect. Now Ockham turns those ideas in God, into signs as well. "To signify men by the word 'man' is nothing else—and contains nothing else—but the word, men and the will's act by which we use that word [to designate, R.S.] men. Otherwise a sign contains nothing. Those acts and those words entail no consequence whatsoever as regards the thing or as regards anything anywhere else ..." (*I Sent.* dist. XXXV, q. 4). The will here stands for what will later be called convention. The phrase 'no consequence as regards anything anywhere else' is less vague than it may seem: the sign entails no real connection to God's idea of what it signifies.

This is another instance of epistemic conceptualism as it results from the battle against universals.[69] Conceptualism means that we generate the concepts by which we signify things (*significata*). It means the eclipse of mediations. You may recall that mediation was precisely what the universalist genius of the neo-Platonist strove on. Proclus' world is entirely a world made of intermediaries and mediations. Now if our concepts cannot address any real universal trait in things, this is because all intermediaries between the thing and us are lacking. The form—principle of what a substance is, as well as principle of the substance known—is lacking and with it, the active intellect extracting the form from the thing to be known. More precisely in epistemological terms: the moment of the phantasm—first moment of abstraction—is lacking. And now the parallel:

- human concepts are representations that are not phantasms, i.e., not *caused by* things; likewise:
- divine ideas are representations that are not models, i.e., not *causes for* things.

Both are established by the will. For humans, that means, by convention; for God: "I demonstrate that the idea is creature itself" (*I Sent.* dist. XXXV, q. 5: *creatura producibilis* [producible creature]).

There is no 'rose' in God's mind, only the simplicity of his willing this rose. It is not in his intellect, for if it were, then God's will would be limited by the reservoir of ideas (*omnitudo realitatum* [totality of realities]). Also, recourse to the rose qua 'producible' in God would grant us knowledge and the producibles would again amount to divine ideas. But God's will is unknowable; therefore the things he wills are equally unknowable. The will signifies things to us, just as we use conventions for signifying and pointing, for ostensive or deictic gestures.

This goes far beyond the classical question of whether there are ideas of singulars in God. Ockham holds: there are no ideas in God, only singulars—directly and immediately creatable. He speaks of God's practical knowledge: "I say that divine knowing concerning the things God can make is practical... Divine production may be termed 'practical' inasmuch as it depends contingently on God's will" (*I Sent.* dist. XXXV, q. 6). He argues the utmost dispersion: God's will is contingent; it may will to produce this rose or to make that proud warrior fall from his horse to his death; God's own knowing is such doing. So, divine knowing is practical, contingent, aimed at singulars. Its content is not eternal law and order, but a collection that can be increased, decreased, modified, replaced.

This, then, singularizes and disperses God's will as well. Stated otherwise, it renders it free—free from any ideal schema that God would set for himself in his mind and then exteriorize *for our comfort* since such an order would embed every being and every occurrence in its place. With Scotus, God becomes entirely *free for* individual causation—one may say: for individual destiny. Ockham applies his razor to the ontological thickness of the world in order to enlarge that space for God's freedom. "God can do things he does not do; indeed, a free cause that acts contingently can do otherwise than it is doing; now God is of such a kind" (*I Sent.* dist. XLIII, q. 1).

IV.

Meister Eckhart's Speculative Mysticism

If in Ockham the Aristotelian heritage is radicalized in its empirical emphasis and in its restriction of universals, Meister Eckhart radicalizes Aristotelianism in quite a different way. In fact, the two key notions that we have worked out in Aquinas—'esse' in ontology, and 'connaturality' in philosophy of knowledge—here serve to articulate a path of assimilation whereby man comes to resemble God and finally discovers himself 'beyond God insofar as God is considered as the Other.' From the notion of 'esse' that we have worked out, it is clear that Eckhart will never speak of substantial identification with God; rather, the process of 'esse' is one and the same in man and in God, he would say. I have indicated occasionally how this possibility is rooted in Aquinas' own teaching, in as much as 'esse' is one, and hence the most universal, and at the same time always singular. This possibility of a process-like identity between man and God had not been pursued by Aquinas, though.

Born about 1260 at Hochheim, Thuringia, studies with Albert the Great in Cologne. The intellectual climate there was entirely dominated by Thomas Aquinas, who had died recently. Eckhart is called 'master' because of that illustrious function—a Master's degree—which he fulfilled in Paris. He occupied many administrative functions in his Order; quite as the Spanish mystics later, he was the opposite of a recluse, actually a very active man. Immensely popular for his preaching, so that when he was brought before the Inquisition, this was a public affair, with published statements, replies, denunciations, etc.... He was tried for heresy first by a Franciscan bishop (unfavorable to OP[70] anyway), then at the Pope's Court at Avignon. The bull of 1329 condemns 28 propositions allegedly made in Eckhart's teachings. The bull speaks of Eckhart as already dead; it states that Eckhart has retracted all errors that he may have taught, and his tomb is unknown. The circumstances of his death are altogether unknown.

"Whenever I preach, I usually speak of detachment [*Abgeschiedenheit*] and that man must become bereft of himself and of all things;

secondly that one should be remodeled into the image of the simple good which is God; thirdly that one should remember the great nobility which God has deposited in the mind in order for man to reach God through it; fourthly of the purity of the divine nature" (DW II, p. 528).[71] I shall follow these four steps of Detachment: Dissimilarity, Similarity, Identity, Breakthrough. *Abegescheidenheit,* in modern German *Abgeschiedenheit,* is formed of the prefix *ab-* which designates a separation *(abetuon:* to rid oneself of something; *abekere:* turning away, apostasy) and of the verb *scheiden* or *gescheiden.* In its transitive form, this verb means 'to isolate,' 'to split,' 'to separate,' and in its intransitive form 'to depart,' 'to die.' The word *abegescheidenheit,* 'detachment' or 'renunciation,' and the verbs of deliverance evoke, in the allusive thought of Meister Eckhart, a mind that is on the way to dispossession from all exteriority which might spoil its serenity.[72]

To understand such an itinerary of existence instructs man about more than himself. Speaking of man engaged on the way of detachment means also to be speaking of God; and of God Meister Eckhart does not speak otherwise than through his praise of the detached man. All that is essential about man and God would have been said if only it were possible to retrace the steps of detachment. Detachment draws the horizon within which God encounters man. The difficulty in interpreting Meister Eckhart stems from the necessity to reproduce in ourselves the disposition that allows such an encounter to occur.

1. Dissimilarity

> All creatures are mere nothingness. I do not say that they are small or anything at all: they are mere nothingness.[73]

Here the dissimilarity between God and man is declared to be absolute—just as absolute as the difference between 'yes' and 'no.' God is, while man, inasmuch as he is created, is not. 'Creature' designates a being that incessantly receives itself from elsewhere; it has received existence, life, and intelligence from another. It does not possess itself, the other is its being, in itself it is nothing.

What does not possess being is nothingness. But no creature has being, for its being depends on the presence of God. Were God to withdraw for an instant from all creatures, they would be annihilated.[74]

From the condition of creature, Eckhart concludes that the created is nothingness. Earlier he spoke in images: "As long as the creature is creature, it carries within itself bitterness and harm, wrong and distress." This is a metaphorical way of stating the nothingness of creaturehood. A short inquiry into Eckhart's vocabulary of being will reveal how we are to understand "nothingness."

Eckhart uses three groups of words for "being." The word *wesen* is the most remarkable because of its semantic broadness. Generally it is used to translate in a verbal manner the being of beings which the Scholastics designated by *ens commune* [being in general]. But it covers a much wider extent and overlaps with "essence." We therefore translate *wesen* either by 'essence' or, according to the context, by 'essential coming forth.' *Wesen* is the word for the totality of what shows itself, under the point of view of its coming forth. The being of beings is thought of as coming continually to the light. Being is thought of as the daybreak over beings.

Conversely, *unwesene* is reserved by Meister Eckhart for that essential coming forth which, at the same time, retreats into concealment, that is, into the darkness in which the acting of the mind is united to the acting of God.

The mind acts in *unwesene*, and it follows God who acts in the *unwesene*.[75]

In a certain sense, *unwesene* could be translated by 'nothingness'; but as it expresses the abolition of the positivity of being, it points, so to speak, not beneath but beyond being, as the *hyper-on* of the neo-Platonists. In the *unwesene* of the Godhead, the activity of the ground of the mind is identical with the actuality of God. *Unwesene*, then, does not apply to creatures. The opposition between being and nothingness in creatures is expressed in a different terminology.

The Middle High German word for 'nothing' is *niht*. It is composed of the particle of negation *ne* and of *iht* 'something' or 'anything whatsoever.' The form is preserved in modern Dutch (*iets*, something; *niets*, nothing). "The creature is nothing." What exactly is it that Eckhart wants to negate in the created? *Iht* is denied; the creature is not 'a something.' *Iht* designates the existing in general: the creature endowed with a borrowed being, the *entitas* [beingness] of the *ens* [being] or the *ousia* [beingness] of the *on* [being]. *Iht* speaks of a being's fact that it is. It denotes that which qualifies thought to represent to itself a being as a being. One is reminded of what Martin Heidegger calls *Seiendheit,* a word which has been translated by "beingness."[76] *Niht* is the negation of the fact of being. The creature in general cannot be represented as being; its *iht* resides in God, not in itself.[77]

(3) We translate *isticheit* by 'primordial being.' *Sîn* and *isticheit* have often the same extension and comprehension:

> God's being is my being and God's primordial being is my primordial being.[78]

"The creature is mere nothingness." *Iht* comes to a thing as God incessantly lavishes being upon his creature. Let God's prodigality of *iht* cease for an instant, and the universal presence of the cosmos will immediately vanish.

> All creatures are with God, and God grants them their essential coming forth together with his presence.[79]

> Outside of God there is nothing but only nothing.[80]

From the viewpoint of the history of doctrines, this entire theme of nothingness and dissimilarity can easily be traced back to Augustine. When Eckhart speaks of *unglîcheit,* the country of dissimilarity,[81] he claims the authority of the *regio dissimilitudinis* [realm of dissimilitude].

It is from here also that the difference between God and man becomes thinkable. The boldness of Eckhart's position clearly appears when one has understood that this difference introduces identity and otherness into man himself: identity with God in the core of the mind, and otherness in the faculties or powers, and in the body. Man is the locus of union and disunion, the Difference between identity and difference. In the 'ground,' man lives in God and God in him; but in his creaturehood, man is of the world. Disunion is rooted in the dissimilarity, in the being-with by which man is 'close to,' therefore removed from God. The difference between God and not-God is a cleft that splits man thoroughly. Only out of this cleft can God, man, and the world be thematized. At this point, it should not surprise us any longer that Eckhart actually abolishes the methodological distinction between theology, anthropology, and cosmology. All these three sciences would have to develop the same opposition between 'in-God' and 'with-God' which is entrusted to man alone. He is at the same time the being-there and the being-elsewhere of the origin; he is among all beings the one that is alike-unlike the origin.

> When the Father engendered all creatures, he brought me forth. I emanated together with all creatures and yet I remain within, in the Father.[82]

"Created" and yet "in the Father": these two determinations do not isolate two entities in man, one divine, the other human; rather they are 'provenance' and 'imminence.'

It aims at an education of seeing:

> He who knew nothing other than creatures would have no need for thinking of sermons, for each creature is full of God and is a book.[83]

If one renounces creatures inasmuch as they are creatures, one's eyes will be opened to God who is hidden in them. Meister Eckhart, "a monk appreciated for his administrative qualities,"[84] did not feel that things deserved no attention at all; however, he considered that only He from whom things hold their being is worthy of interest in them. Every creature is to the credit of the Creator and not to its own credit. Here again, the thrust of the argument is not 'indicative,' but 'imperative.'

The 'indicative' thought treats of substances, and by stressing their independence and sufficiency of being it assigns to man his place within the universal order. Indicative thought ponders what is given; therefore it is *old* by nature. 'Imperative' thought, on the other hand, even though it can call on a tradition as ancient as

Socrates, is essentially *new* since it addresses the hearer who has become ready to turn around on his road. This is the protreptic meaning of Eckhart's statement that "the being of the world is to receive being." The being of the world is radically dependent, insufficient; thus the union with the One requires a negation (detachment) of the negation (creature).

2. Similarity

God's endeavor is to give himself to us entirely. Just as fire seeks to draw the wood into itself and itself into the wood, it first finds the wood unlike itself. It takes a little time. Fire begins by warming it, then heating it, and then it smokes and crackles because the two are so unlike each other. The hotter the wood becomes, the more still and quiet it grows. The more it is likened to the fire, the more peaceful it is, until it becomes entirely flame. That the wood be transformed into fire, all dissimilarity must be chased out of it.[85]

We recognize in this text the strategy of detachment: from dissimilarity to similarity, and from similarity to union. The sermon "Jesus Entered" in this regard invoked the axiom: "the likeness of the like alone is the basis of union." The comparison with the fire which, by assimilation, attracts the ignitable to the perfection of the ignited, suggests a slow growth: in order for the blaze to absorb the wood, "it takes a little time." The wood is reborn 'son' of the blaze, by *gelîcheit* [likeness]. When the absorption is completed, it will be distinct from the fire by its very indistinction, as the Son is alike-unlike the Father. The wood will be the perfect image of the fire:

Nothing is so much alike and unlike at the same time ... as God and the creature. What is there indeed so unlike and like each other as these whose unlikeness is their very likeness, whose indistinction is distinction itself? ... Being distinct by indistinction, it resembles by dissimilarity. The more it is unlike, the more it is alike.[86]

The like and the unlike are resolved by flames and incandescences. Assimilation spreads the glory of that to which we are likened:

because of the nature of its constituents, dissimilarity overcomes itself into similarity, and likeness shines into unlikeness. Beyond this:

> An image is not of itself; nor is it for itself. It has its origin in that of which it is the image. To that it belongs properly with all that it is. It does not belong to what is foreign to this origin, nor does it owe anything to this. An image receives its being immediately from that of which it is an image. It has one being with it and it is the same being.[87]

The repose in which a detached man already lives means that "with all that he is" he belongs to Him whom he reflects as an image. With Him he "has one being and is the same being." As to the not-yet that separates similarity from perfect identity, Eckhart says:

> You often ask how you should live. Note this carefully. See what has just been said of the image: in exactly the same way you should live. You should be in him and for him, and not in yourself and for yourself.[88]

Such an understanding of similarity begins a dialectical process in which the being in and for God consumes the being in itself and for itself. Just as fire "makes everything run towards its first simplicity,"[89] so detachment incinerates the old man, that is, the created man in man, who does not carry the imprint of the image of God. The conquest of resemblance with the origin passes through the abandonment of all created likeness. When man will be *ungelîch,* unlike the created and totally *entglîchet,* no longer resembling anything, then he will be like God.

Eckhart's speculation on the being of images echoes the patristic ponderings on the same subject. Imagine a man standing before a mirror. Properly speaking, where does the image that absorbs his attention reside? Does its being inhere in the body from which it emanates, or rather in the reflection which he contemplates? "The image is in me, of me, towards me," answers Eckhart.[90] Were I to move back a step, the image would no longer be.

Every image has two properties. The first is that it receives its being immediately from that of which it is an image, without interference of the will.

Its outgoing is indeed natural, and it thrusts itself out of nature like a branch from the tree. When an image is cast on a mirror, our face will be reflected in it whether it likes it or not... The second property of the image is to be observed in the similarity of the image.[91]

The first point accords with the conclusion on created being: the image has no proper being, being comes to it from another, it does not exist originarily. The image exists only in its "outgoing" *(ûzganc)*. The second point explains from where it extracts its being: it is nothing else but that very dependence we call reflection. Eckhart applies these considerations to the relationship between man and God. Man, as an image of God, remains 'with' him of whom he is the image, distinct from him and not 'in' him. In its outgoing, the image stays at the periphery of the origin.

He draws perhaps too radical a distinction between the mind as an image of God and creation in general; conversely, he does not distinguish the mind enough from the divine Persons. Like the Son and the Spirit, the mind is defined by its *ad* [to], which establishes it near to God. Just as Christ is with the Father, the detached man should be with Christ, in turn engendering the unique Word which he becomes himself. Then the assimilation will be perfect. In the sermon on Justice, Eckhart illustrates this teaching by the proximity of Eve to Adam:

> The just live eternally "with God," directly with God, neither below nor above. They accomplish all their works with God, and God accomplishes his own with them. Saint John says: "The Word was with God." It was totally alike and next to him, neither below nor above but alike. When God created man, he drew woman from the rib of man, so that woman was alike to man. He made her neither from the head nor from the feet, so that she would be neither above nor below man, but that she would be equal to him. Likewise the just mind is to be equal with God and next to him: exactly alike, neither inferior nor superior to him.[92]

The Word is with God (*bî gote*), Eve was with Adam, the just man is with Justice: likewise the man devoid of all created images is with God and is the image of God. We must become ad-verb to the Verb.

3. Identity

Dissimilarity and Similarity have to be surpassed into Identity:

> Scripture says that we have to become like God (1 John 3:2). 'Like,' the word is bad and deceptive. If I liken myself to someone else, and if I find someone who is like me, then this man behaves as if he were I, although he is not and deceives people about it. Many things look like gold, but since they are not, they lie. In the same way all things pretend to be like God; but they are lying, since they are not like him. God can no more suffer likeness than he can suffer not being God. Likeness is something that does not occur in God; what does occur in the Godhead and in eternity is oneness. But likeness is not oneness [*glîcheit enist niht ein*]. Whenever I am one with something, I am not like it. There is nothing alien in oneness. In eternity there is only oneness, but not likeness.[93]

Eckhart illustrates his conception of identity through the example of fire: when everything combustible has been absorbed, fire passes beyond dissimilarity and similarity. It blazes, becoming "entirely one single and unique flame,"[94] "heat and conflagration,"[95] which "always seeks the One."[96] It does not seek likeness, which is created, but the One: *ein unglîch*.[97] Combustion, carried out by the fire and undergone by the wood, results in identity. Eckhart calls this identity *ein im gewürke*, identical in operation. Such identity or oneness terminates the cataphasis of detachment. The apophasis, further on, will lead us beyond this concatenation by fire.

> Acting and becoming are one. God and I are one in this work: he acts and I become. Fire transforms all things it touches into its own nature. The wood does not change the fire into itself, but the fire changes the wood into itself. In the same way we are transformed into God so that we may know him as he is.[98]

Fire and light are frequent metaphors for oneness in Meister Eckhart. He also uses the example of vision. Just as light projected on a colored surface becomes one with it and shines in identical clarity with it, so in perfect availability to the will of God I become one with the Father. From this unity emanates all identical incandescence, the Son. The philosophical importance of Meister Eckhart lies in his transformation of the understanding of being, as illustrated here.

Appeal could also be made to the example of music. The hearer of such melodious beauty is "all ears." If he does not know how to reproduce inwardly, simultaneously, identically, that which his ears hear, if by distraction or incapacity he omits to accompany in himself the sounds that the senses perceive, then he does not know how to listen. Properly speaking, perfect listening implies that the distinction between the soloist, on one side, and the listener, on the other, is no longer true. Through the unique event of the song which enraptures us, one identical being accomplishes itself: energetic identity. The same operative identity appears in conversation: the 'we,' there, is not the achievement of 'I' or 'you,' but two beings are determined as identical: identical in the 'gewürke,' i.e. in an event. Such is the transformation of Aquinas' notion of act (*energeia*) in Meister Eckhart.

The pattern for Meister Eckhart's understanding of being as operative, energetic identity is clear: Aristotle's metaphysics of knowledge. 'Actual' identity is opposed to the identity of substances. This latter identity is the one that metaphysics and its offspring, pantheism, deal with. It is quite clear that Eckhart had overcome representation of substances. Because he preached out of another form of thought, he was condemned as a heretic. Metaphysical representation admits of no other identity than that of substances with themselves: the ontic identity of a thing that remains itself. In objection to our interpretation of energetic identity as the rise of the 'we' in the event of a dialogue or of the harmony between the soloist and his hearer, representational thought would reply: substances are '*simpliciter diversa*' [simply diverse]; otherness remains the first and inescapable fact in any relation. To Eckhart's teaching of the simultaneous begetting of the Word it has been objecting for six centuries that God and man are ontologically distinct beings. Indeed, out of Aristotle's metaphysics of knowledge, Eckhart declares: I give birth to the Word together with the Father, and I am that Word, neither more nor less: in being, substance, and nature.

From the foregoing it results that there are two conflicting ways or orders of understanding identity: that of being as a process and that of being as substance. We have already hit upon this conflict.

In a 'verbal' understanding of being, one will emphasize energetic identity, while in a 'nominal' understanding of being, one will speak of substantial or ontic identity. Meister Eckhart's understanding of being is 'verbal' and that of identity, 'energetic.'

> As long as any difference pertaining to created things gets response in the mind, it thereby feels chagrin. I repeat what I have already said on many occasions: as far as the mind's natural and created being goes, there is no truth. I say that there is something which is beyond the created nature of the mind. Many priests, however, do not grasp that there is something so closely related to God and so identical with him... A man who is thus borne above all light dwells in unity.[99]

Living in the light beyond light, man no longer lives 'with' God but 'in' him:

> God is not found in distinction. When the mind reaches the original image [of which it is a reflection, R.S.] and finds itself alone in it, then it finds God. Finding itself and finding God is one single process, outside of time. As far as it penetrates into him, it is identical with God, ... not included, nor united, but more: identical.[100]

Identical is the event as God begets me as himself and begets himself as me. He begets me as his essential being and as his nature. There is one life and one essential being and one work there.[101]

> The ground of the mind and the ground of God are one sole essential being.[102]

Eckhart wants so much to insist on this energetic identity between God and man that he does not hesitate to accumulate adjectives against all customary usage: *ein einic ein ungeschieden*,[103] one unique unity without difference.

Exclusion of the multiple and of difference in Eckhart is possible because he speaks of identity as an event, birth, or breakthrough. For such thinking a few customary categories of representation turn out to be inadequate, in particular the opposition between transcendence and immanence. Identity as transcendence would infringe on the Eckhartian principle of exclusion of all mediations from God; identity as immanence would rehabilitate the being of creatures and would thus weaken the ontophanic project of detachment. It is on the identity of the totality, the energetic identity of God, man, and the world, that we find some of the most astonishing statements that Meister Eckhart has left us.

> God gives to all things equally, and as they flow from God, they are all equal. Indeed, angels and men and creatures are equal in their primitive emanation, by which they flow from God. Someone who would get hold of things in their primitive emanation would get hold of them as they are all equal. If they are thus equal in time, they are still more so in eternity, in God. If we take a fly, in God, it is more noble in God than the highest angel is in itself. This is how all things are equal in God and are God himself.[104]

The last sentence expresses a kind of axiom dear to Eckhart which is found in different forms in his sermons: "All that is in God is God."[105] "In God, no creature is more noble than the other." "In God, there is nothing but God." "What is in the first, is the first." "What is in the One is the One." These propositions can be read in reference to the preexistence of the soul. But that is not the entire story: it is releasement that accounts for the restorative, new birth of all things to identity. Energetic identity is thus more primitive and, as it is uncreated, more real than substantial identity. Likewise releasement is more primitive, uncreated, than detachment, whose function is to regulate man's dealings with things, that is, created substances.

The identity of the totality is here neither transcendence made immanence (metaphysical identity) nor universal ontic homogeneity (pantheistic identity), but playful presence ('symbolic' identity). God, man, and the world are joined together by the play of this identity. The mind devoid of all *eigenschaft* [property] is the 'there' of their threefold intercourse. He who renounces himself entirely and reinstates the ancient void of images, by his serenity, sets the threefold free and grounds their identity on play.[106] Man is the field where the threefold appears, unendingly dislocated as long as he turns himself towards nothingness, but reunited in their first identity when he commits himself to *gelâzenheit* [releasement].

The true nobility of the ground of the mind lies in that a released man becomes the locus where the energetic identity of God, of himself, and of the world, produces itself. According to the cipher of unity, the universe is genuinely 'universe,' that is, a turning towards the One, only in a released man. "What is in the One is the One." According to the cipher of truth, releasement leads beings back to their primitive 'connaturality,' gathered into the same divine nature.[107]

4. Breakthrough

It is in the name of the strictness of releasement that Meister Eckhart criticizes the pretension of the supreme being, 'God,' to the rank of the origin. The supreme being has still a 'why,' namely all other beings. We speak of God as the highest reason behind life. We speak even of his will and his intention. But intentionality and purpose have no place in releasement. To think of God divinely is to render his ebullience aimless.

The identity of the three is effected by the free unfolding of an existence that has left everything and that therefore lets everything be. This effecting and this unfolding, Meister Eckhart says, can be compared to the pace of a stallion launched at full speed over spacious grassland: its nature will urge it to expend itself in galloping and leaping as much as its strength will allow. In this way it finds its happiness.[108] We could ask: why does it run? It runs in order to run, without a why. Likewise the identity of the threefold accomplishes itself for its own sake, without a why.

"Why do you love God?" — "I do not know, because of God." — "Why do you love the truth?" — "Because of the truth." — "Why do you love justice?" — "Because of justice." — "Why do you love goodness?" — "Because of goodness." — "Why do you live?" — "My word! I do not know! But I am happy to live."[109]

God is, man lives, things subsist and perish—all this without a why. Eckhart expresses this in multiple ways. His meditation on the why is an unveiling. God, man, and the world unveil themselves in their first 'dehiscence' (*uzbruch, Ausbruch* [literally, breaking out] or *uzvluz, Ausfluss* [literally, flowing out]) from their origin, without a why. The last question actually remains unanswered: instead of an answer, a response is given. An answer exhibits some knowledge, but a response involves the entire human being.

What is the sense of a quest which seeks an origin beyond God? The metaphysician will object that beyond God, the highest being, no origin can be thought. But are the new birth and releasement thinkable as long as the excellence of God is in this way objectified? If God is represented as the duplicate beyond or within man, that is, as the Perfect above our imperfection, the divine birth can only be represented by sacrificing either identity to difference (God as the partner of the soul, Pietism) or difference to identity (God as the oceanic substance which swallows up the soul, Pantheism). Meister Eckhart, however, maintains both identity and difference. He attempts to think the origin prior to the manifestation of the threefold. To do so, he turns towards man as that being who needs only to come back to himself for the question of the origin to be raised. There is no path other than releasement that can overcome God represented as the highest being. Living 'sunder warumbe,' without why, is to let go all exterior motivation. The God whom this other way of thinking annihilates in his function of foundation is indeed the God of western Christianity. If you seek God for the sake of a foundation, Eckhart says, if you look for God even for the sake of God himself, then

> you behave as though you transformed God into a candle in order to find something with it; and when one has found what one looks for, one throws away the candle.[110]

However, to "look for nothing" is neither subversion nor absurdity. Meister Eckhart only draws the ultimate consequence of letting-be. What is, let it be. Everything could as well not be, but since it is, let it be. God, man, and the world could not be, but since they are, let them be. "Those who seek something with their works, those who act for a why, are serfs and mercenaries."

As the *archē*, the origin as wherefrom (represented by the words 'since they are'), is without a why, so, too, the *telos*, the origin as whereto (represented by the words 'let them be') is without a why. For Eckhart, such thought leads man into the desert, which is prior to God, man, and the world.

> I have spoken of a power in the mind. In its first manifestation, it does not apprehend God. It does not apprehend him insofar as he is good, nor insofar as he is the truth. It penetrates into the ground, it pursues and burrows, and it apprehends God in his oneness and in his desert *(einoede)*; it apprehends God in his wilderness *(wüstunge)* and in his own ground.[111]

The outcome of the mind's breakthrough is that "Got entwird" [God unbecomes]. God acts, but to the *Godhead* every operation is foreign. Operation is of the order of consequences. The desert is not fertile in anything: likewise the Godhead is arid; it does not create anything. In the desert everything begins only: but God disappears. The desert is the vast solitude, there is no place for two in the desert. The opposition between a Creator and a creature vanishes. In the desert, entreaties are of no avail; there is no opposite of man towards whom he might raise his hands. In the desert, the wind and the sand wipe out the traces of the caravans: the steps of God disappear together with those of man and the world. "God and Godhead are as distinct as heaven and earth."

The desert is full of seeds but they do not sprout there. The Godhead is a house, Eckhart says, full of people but from which no one as of yet has gone out. Let the dwellers go out into the street and they will be hailed: 'God,' 'Eckhart' ...

> God becomes; where all creatures enunciate God, there God becomes. When I still stood in the ground, the soil, the river, and the source of the Godhead, no one asked me where I was going or what I was doing. There was no one there to question me. But when I went out by dehiscence, all creatures cried out: "God." If someone were to ask me: "Brother Eckhart, when did you leave home?" this would indicate that I must previously have been inside. It is thus that all creatures speak of God. And why do they not speak of the Godhead? Everything that is in the Godhead is one, and of this nothing can be said.[112]

Whoever speaks of God intends to speak of his most sublime counterpart, that is, of a being opposable to other beings. He invokes him as the one who saves, the one who judges, who acts ... always as the Other.

The 'Godhead' refers to the fullness of ideas in which there is no other. "'Virgin' designates a human who is devoid of all foreign images and who is as void as he was when he was not yet," that is, when he still dwelt within the Godhead.

> When I still stood in my first cause, I had no God, I was cause of myself... But when by free will I went out and received my created being, then I had a God. Indeed, before there were creatures, God was not yet God, but he was what he was.[113]

He was what he was: the origin is radically unknowable. The expression "I was cause of myself" is very strong: according to the traditional teaching God alone is *causa sui* [cause of himself]. Here it is applied to man. It has to be understood according to the axiom of identity: in the first cause, everything is first cause. The sermon "Blessed Are the Poor" continues:

> This is why I pray to God to rid me of God, for my essential being [*mîn wesenlich wesen*] is above God insofar as we comprehend God as the principle of creatures. Indeed, in God's own being, where God is raised above all being and all distinctions, I was myself, I willed myself, and knew myself to create this man [that I am, R.S.]. Therefore I am cause of myself according to my being which is eternal, but not according to my becoming which is temporal. Therefore also I am unborn, and according to my unborn being I can never die. According to my unborn being I have always been, I am now, and shall eternally remain. What I am by my [temporal, R.S.] birth is to die and be annihilated, for it is mortal; therefore with time it must pass away. In my [eternal, R.S.] birth all things were born, and I was cause of myself as well as of all things. If I had willed it, neither I nor any things would be. And if I myself were not, God would not be either: that God is God, of this I am a cause. If I were not, God would not be God. There is, however, no need to understand this.[114]

I do not reflect God, I do not reproduce him, I declare him.

God, then, undergoes the same fate as things, that is, they perish. The Godhead, on the other hand, is not a something. Every 'thing' has to disappear with time, for it belongs to the day. 'Thing' designates beings in their determinate existence. One way to cancel that determinacy is to oppose it to indeterminacy as contingency to necessity.

The idea that God 'must' love man, *got muoz,* is frequent in his writings.[115]

> I will never thank God that he loves me, for he cannot do otherwise, whether he wishes it or not; his nature forces him to it. I will rather thank him that in his goodness he cannot cease loving me.[116]

'God loves us'; this describes a relation of exteriority between subjects that are capable of love. 'I thank God because he loves me,' then, expresses the love one person shows to another person in testimony of reciprocity. Representational thinking declares: 'God loves me.' On the other hand, 'God must love me' intends to abolish the representable relationship of exteriority: reciprocity falls, and every relation between persons or subjects passes away. We are borne not by God's love, but by his having-to-love, that is, by his nature. God's nature is that he loves; God is love.

The intrinsic necessity which a being obeys lies in its nature. If God necessarily bears us in his love, then he bears us in his nature or his Godhead. 'God must' is a way for Eckhart to intimate the origin. 'God must love us': in a love so lavished, God vanishes. 'God' is the name for someone who loves me because he freely chooses to do so. But by his nature, God loves me beyond all choosing and willing. He introduces me to that realm where he ceases to be God, namely, into the desert of his primordial *wesen* [essential unfolding]. Only then am I loved necessarily, but no one is there to love me.

"'Life' means a kind of seething in which a thing ferments and first pours itself into itself [*bullitio*], all that it is into all that it is, before spilling over and pouring itself outside [*ebullitio*]."[117] Before things come to appear, they are 'teeming' with a respiration without a why in the bosom of the Godhead. If we call the act of expiration, by which created things are diffused outside, their 'origin,' then the tranquil intra-divine respiration that precedes creation will have to be called a 'pre-originary' origin. This is meant by the word *ursprunc* [origin]: an actuality prior to God in which life diffuses "all that it is into all that it is." The pre-originary origin is animated throughout by one single and identical breath. Everything that breathes in the origin is the origin.

Properly speaking, however, the pre-originary origin *is* not. If it were, its being would make it opposable to other beings; it would have to be the God of the metaphysical tradition. For Eckhart *ursprunc* (*archē*) is not the beginning of being; rather it is nothingness and anarchy. The *ursprunc* is nothingness. Previously we have said: creatures are nothingness.

> All things have been drawn from nothingness; this is why their true origin [*ursprunc*] is nothingness.[118]

The departure as well as the arrival of detachment is nothingness. From foliation to dehiscence, the fruit of detachment 'nihilates.' The *ursprunc* as anarchy breaks the fetters of individuation and rids me of all attachments and links, even of God. Through such riddance I become as free as I was when I was universal nothingness in the Godhead.

> When this will turns for an instant away from itself, and returns to its first origin [*in sînen êrsten ursprunc*], then the will recovers its proper free fashion, and it is free.[119]

In its pre-originary origin the will sets itself loose from any principle; it is anarchic. Nothing precedes it; therefore it has nothing to obey, except itself. Detachment, at this stage, ignores or suspends any reference to determinate being. Man is perfectly released. He exists himself as the pre-originary origin, he is the origin of the origin, and no one can lay restrictions upon his freedom, not even God. The order of commanding and obeying is reversed:

> The humble man does not solicit [*bitten*] anything [from God, R.S.], but he can indeed command [*gebieten*] him.[120]

An existence that dwells in nothingness is one in which everything just begins. It abides in the origin of the Creator. In this pre-originary origin, says Meister Eckhart, only silence maintains itself.[121]

At the outset of his odyssey of detachment, man did not expect that much. His path appeared as one of voluntary poverty, but now it has led him into a region beyond God where he does not recognize himself any longer. He feels as if he had reached that point of wandering that Japanese Zen masters depict by a canvas totally covered with black:[122] God, man, and the world are no more, there is only the unspeakable intra-divine 'ebullience' without a purpose and in which nothing lasts. But his wandering exploration of the origin has changed him. He has become playful. He asks no more for meanings and goals. Breakthrough goes a step further. The three subsist no longer; they allude to a oneness that preserves the manifold in the unity of provenance and imminence.

A man who has experienced this breakthrough, Meister Eckhart says, goes back to the businesses of the world: the stable or some other trade. He is no longer eager to hold God; he knows that eagerness, even mystical, makes one forgetful. Eagerness wants to get hold of God as though to envelop his head in a cloak and put him away under a bench.[123]

5. Meister Eckhart on analogy

You remember the development that Aristotelian analogy underwent in Aquinas: from predicamental analogy—the relation of being between substance and accidents—Aquinas stepped to what we would have to call the transcendental analogy of being. Any analogy constitutes a unity of order by reference to a first. Such unity allows for a diversity within the order so constituted, and at the same time the diversity is not irreducible. Analogy thus stands between equivocity and univocity. In Aquinas the order obtains, not only between substance and accidents, but first of all between the created and the Creator: there is a hierarchy *of* substances. In Aquinas, thus, analogy is grounded on creative causality; it applies to a relation 'unius ad alterum' [of one to the other]; it is the technical way of stating the production of being and its appropriation according to deficient similarity. This analogy is called transcendental because the terms so communicated are the transcendental perfections of being.

But communication of perfections so organized, requires a bearer—not a *suppositum* [supposit] (and that was Aquinas' philosophical contribution), but an act. The analogy between Creator and created was a communication of actuality, not simply of perfections. The perfections were seen as concomitant with the communication of actuality.

What, now, is Eckhart's position on analogy? The question is all the more burning since he explicitly wants to eliminate any intermediary, any difference in a way, between Creator and created. Everything hinges, then, on his version of 'actuality'; i.e. he can escape a conflation of Creator and created into one single fabric only if the language of *energeia* [actuality] prevails. This, we have seen, is achieved through the metaphors of 'birth of the Word in the mind' and 'Breakthrough beyond God.'

Nevertheless, let us look at the traditional aspect of analogy in Meister Eckhart. He uses again and again the example of justice to show a certain communion between man and God. But one has to see that ultimately, in Eckhart's intellectual universe, the theory of analogy is insufficient to give an account of being. He explicates his theory of analogy in his commentary on the biblical verse, "Those who eat me will hunger still" [Micah 6:14]. The creature feeds on God for its being, he says, and it always has hunger for him since its being never becomes its own, but comes from another.

Any analogical perfection, not only justice but also being, will naturally be prior to all that is created. The being of things created springs from the first cause without any mediation. This cause alone is: *Esse est Deus,* being is God.[124] Even when limited in a particular being, these perfections remain general perfections; that is, they remain God. Beings exist by virtue of that being which is God; beings are just, good, true, by virtue of justice, goodness, truth, all of which are God. Thus, the concrete, individualized transcendental always expresses the abstract, universal transcendental. Not only is each transcendental, convertible with every other, God, but it is God himself even in the finite mode in which a particular being realizes it, in 'this and that.'

The structure of the act-to-be of beings is not measured by, but identified with the one being that is God. Thomas was careful to maintain a more radical difference between God and things: he taught that they are alike and unlike God as being is communicated to them by decreasing intensity and increasing limitation. Eckhart destroys the concept of an analogy by deficient similarity and limitation: if being is God, then beings are what they are entirely in God and by God; outside of God they are nothingness. Much more, insofar as they are, they are God. Insofar as man is just, he is justice.

The construction of a proportionality inspired by the predicamental analogy between the substance and its accidents is thus rejected by Eckhart. Under this particular point of view his metaphysics is neither Aristotelian nor Thomist, but neo-Platonic. He considers things not 'from below,' starting with the sensible world, but 'from above,' starting with God. On the other hand, his destruction of all intermediaries between God and the world, the elimination of justice, goodness, truth, etc., as ideas or prototypes subsisting by themselves, estranges him also from neo-Platonic systems. Plotinus, Proclus, Dionysius, and Erigena have in common at least a certain realism of universals. To Eckhart, there is no intermediary that can resist the effectiveness of releasement. Gilson has gone so far as to call the perfections, in Eckhart's thinking, simply "imputed" to the created.[125] Eckhart himself speaks rather of 'borrowing.' Being and all perfections are allotted to the created things *ze borge*, on loan.[126]

"The identical being and the identical substance and nature" that God is himself: what else is there that we could be, since all being is God? The act that makes each thing exist is God's; outside of God no perfection subsists. For Aristotle, the accident is still a certain *on*, an additional entity; for Thomas, too, the created is a being in its own right; *esse* [being] designates first of all the finite sensible substance—so much so that the finite being enjoys a definite autonomy with regard to the divine *ipsum esse* [being itself]. Both philosophers understand being as appropriated according to different degrees of perfection. This is not so for Eckhart. The radicalism of releasement allows for nothing but perfect appropriation: God appropriates man to Himself, perfectly, by imputing to him the being that He is himself. Man points to God in the same way as a crown of vine leaves at the entrance of a tavern points to the wine:[127] without participation and by an extrinsic relationship. Being, that is, God, is 'in the mind,' not 'of the mind.' The gap between the mind's being and the rest of man reduces our ontological autonomy (not our freedom of choice) to nothingness.

Everything created should be loved for the sake of God, not for its own sake. To love things for themselves is indeed to love nothingness and to become nothingness. The analogy between God and man appears 'intentional' (*secundum intentionem tantum*), as a signalization.

Eckhart expands the Aristotelian 'predicamental' analogy or analogy of attribution to God: everything other than God is His 'attribute.' Only the analogy of attribution allows us to think the identity of what is participated with what participates; it is the identity of a transcendental quality in itself and as it is imputed 'on loan' to a finite creature. Thus Eckhart practices a realism that is neither the Aristotelian and Thomist realism of the sub-lunar, nor the Platonic or Platonist realism of universals.

Compared with the Aristotelian tradition, Eckhart's ontology is thus characterized by the fleetingness of borrowed being—evanescent like a ray of the sun in the air—as opposed to the permanence, the duration, and the autonomy of analogical beings according to Thomas. In such a vision of precarious being, the concept of transcendental analogy loses its meaning. One sole and same determination is found at all levels of the analogy: the perfection of the first.[128] Being is formally and numerically one. To be 'this or that' adds nothing to being; the individuation of the just man adds nothing to justice.[129] His realism is a 'mystical realism' according to which only the first analogate is real. The uncreated possesses everything, and the created, nothing.

Does such a theocentrism—some say: such a monism of being— abolish all analogical relations between being, which is God, and created beings? Is there still place for analogy when the created order loses all autonomy? Yes: being qua being, as well as all transcendental perfections, are encountered formally only in the First; but they are encountered also in the derived analogates.

The relation between prime and secondary analogate is one of exteriority and of contradiction: the relation between uncreated and created is exterior because being does not really take root in the created, contradictory because being can belong only to one of the terms. This point can be schematically illustrated by Erigena's classification of four realms of being. To the question 'What is being?,' a neo-Platonist would reply: 'The nature that is not created, but which creates,' as well as 'the natures that are created and create,' that is, the ideas or prototypes; an Aristotelian would reply (although not in this language): 'The nature that is created, but does not create,' that is, finite things. But Eckhart would say: 'The nature that neither is created nor creates'—God's being, the Godhead, into which releasement returns.

The Scholastic theory of analogy is derived from Aristotelian ousiology and neo-Platonic cosmology; but Eckhart's understanding of being can be reduced to neither of these, and actually transcends both. The vocabulary of analogy is therefore in itself and necessarily incapable of making us grasp his ontology at its core. This radical insufficiency is the core of what is called 'speculative mysticism.' Its argument is nevertheless clear: being is not mine; "if I take it from another, it is not mine; rather it has to belong to him from whom I take it."

6. The limits of the analogical understanding of being

a. — Throughout our interpretation of Eckhart we have adopted a single hermeneutical criterion in order to discover his authentic thought beneath the currents of doctrines which intersect in his teaching. This single criterion is the imperative, incitive call to perfect detachment, that is, to releasement. "Rid yourself of all that is yours and give yourself over to God, then God belongs to you as he belongs to himself." Does the analogy of attribution verify this crucial role of releasement?

Yes and no. To understand being as incessantly bestowed upon beings without ever taking root in them certainly reflects an ancient and beautiful vision of things: being is granted in a process, in a continuous outpouring from the Source, and any existence is possible only in the life-giving stream of this procession. This is how the neo-Platonists viewed the cosmos, and assuredly Eckhart is of their lineage. Furthermore, just as Plotinus and his followers taught, so

Eckhart seems to preach an interior asceticism in order to reascend the sequence of emanations and draw life from where it originates. Thus understood, analogy of attribution undeniably resembles the call to active releasement. Nevertheless, releasement is something quite different than a matter of metaphysical speculation. The analogical system cannot give a sufficient place to releasement, which is the simple and single intent behind Eckhart's teaching, and of which ontology is a consequence.

b. — Furthermore, analogy does not satisfy the energetic notion of being: "His knowledge is mine, exactly the same, one sole and identical knowledge: in the master as he teaches, and in the disciple as he is taught." Being had appeared to us as an energetic identity, *einheit im gewürke.* "Acting and becoming are one. God and I are one in operation: he acts and I become." This identity, not of a substantial 'suppositum' [supposit] but of event, is the place from which the question of being has to be raised. *Energeia* [Actuality] is the other side of releasement: no longer peregrination, but union; no longer voluntary detachment, but fulfillment beyond all human faculties. Something like an identity by process is traditionally thinkable only in two cases: with regard to knowledge or with regard to the act to be through which a being that does not exist by itself participates a being that exists by itself. But being, in Meister Eckhart, precisely excludes distinctions such as those between the knowing subject and the object known, and between first act and second act. Being as *einheit im gewürke* requires an intelligibility other than what the systems derived from Plato and Aristotle can offer. It is our understanding that ultimately Eckhart's ontology is irreducible to these two currents in philosophy. Our second objection, then, is that analogy of attribution does not honor the eminent place that the sermon "See What Love" reserves for being as *energeia,* taken in the precise sense of birth and breakthrough.[130]

c. — Fundamentally, it is insufficient to see 'wesen' as the simple equivalent of 'esse.' There is a nuance of process in *Wesen,* which means 'essential presencing' and 'essential coming forth.' When being is called *wesene,* this suggests a coming forth that lasts, the instauration of a dwelling. It is true that the analogy of attribution excludes neither of these two aspects: uncreated and uncreatable being is incessantly granted from elsewhere, and it fixes the created in its dwellings. But to speak of analogy is to represent relations between at least two proportionate terms. Eckhart wants to do away with any such definable proportion as he thinks of one sole and unique breaking forth of whatever is: *wesene,* coming, dwelling. It is understandable that in this line of thought *wesene* swallows up *iht* [something]:

> As long as there is any *iht* within the *wesene* of a thing, this thing is not recreated.[131]

It is also understandable that *wesene* should be the proper name of God:

> "I am": here [the text, R.S.] speaks of *wesene.* The masters say: all creatures can very well say "I"; this is a universal word. But the word *sum,* "am," is different: no one can pronounce it properly except God alone.[132]

d. — The third group of words, *istic* and *isticheit* or *istikeit,* all derived from the verb *sîn* [to be], applies still more exclusively to God. 'Istic' designates something like an intensity of being: "God is 'istiger' [more intensely present] to all creatures than the creature to itself." The distinction between immanence and transcendence vanishes together with the hierarchy of analogically decipherable degrees. If releasement and presence are to be the most acceptable titles for being, then being can no longer be represented as the universal foundation or the inherent reason of all things. A perfectly released man literally represents nothing. Being as presence and as nothingness arises on the path which Eckhart describes as that of solitude, of the desert, and of forgetfulness. Both the philosopher of analogical identity and the thinker of peregrine identity articulate some kind of presence.

Being as coming forth and as a process (*wesene*), as a presence that is nothingness (*isticheit*) directs us away from theories of analogy. — And there are still more reasons to look for a new direction in analyzing Eckhart's concept of being. One has to see that there are experiences of thinking that render traditional categories obsolete—not false, but unable to account for what has to be thought. There are many cases in the history of philosophy where the decisive thinkers *had* to break with received terminologies.

e. — Another departure from analogy is due to Eckhart's intellectualism. He says that the intellect breaks through beyond God into his ground and that the highest name that he can give to God is 'intelligence'. What exactly is at stake in such an identification between God's act to be and his act to know? Under the title *God is Intelligence* Eckhart writes:

> Some say that being, life, and intelligence can be viewed in two ways: firstly in themselves, in which case being is first, life second, and intelligence third; secondly in relation to that which participates them, and then intelligence is first, life second, and being third. But I believe the exact opposite to be true. "In the beginning was the Word" (St. John), which belongs entirely to intelligence. Consequently, among perfections in themselves intelligence comes first, and then determinate or indeterminate being... On the basis of this I show that in God there is no being, determinate or indeterminate. Indeed, if a cause is a true cause, nothing is formally both in the cause and in its effect. Now, since God is the cause of all being, it follows that being is not formally in God. Of course if you wish to call intelligence being, that is agreeable to me. Nevertheless I say that if there is anything in God that you want to call being, it belongs to him through his intelligence.[133]

If in God you wish to call intelligence 'being,' that is agreeable to me! What is at stake is self-possession. In knowing himself, God possesses himself totally. If being, as a synonym for intelligence, is 'agreeable,' then the emphasis in Eckhart's ontology has to lie on the movement of self-appropriation. As pure intelligence, God is entirely transparent to himself. Everything else is either appropriated by him (things created in general) or appropriates him (man in particular). The Christian doctrine of the uncreated Logos (Word), in this reinterpretation according to the dynamics of releasement, becomes a doctrine of being as a process. The utterance of a word, Eckhart says, is a matter of the intellect. God pronounces his Word from all eternity; and man does what God does: "Announce the Word, pronounce it, produce it, bring forth the Word!"[134] Thus man enters the being of God, that is, God's self-possession by his intelligence and by the utterance of his ineffable Word. When man becomes an 'adverb' (*bîwort*) to the 'Verb' (*wort*), he takes possession of God through what is the proper activity of an intellect, namely to pronounce a word. We actually know that in Eckhart God's utterance and mine are identical: "If I were not, God would not be either: that God is God, of this I am a cause. If I were not, God would not be God."[135]

Such a verification of Eckhart's intellectualism by means of releasement, shows clearly why Aristotelian analogy has to be left behind: analogy provides no conceptual tool to articulate self-appropriation as the common 'ground' of God and man.

f. — What actually happens in Meister Eckhart is the failure of God conceived as the cause and reason of beings. Releasement has nothing to count or to base itself upon. When the origin is thought of as the word, or as intelligence, all metaphysical buttresses become provisional. The word speaks, but it does not pose anything. It does not pose itself under beings as their foundation: it supports nothing; and further it does not precede beings as their cause; it presupposes nothing. The origin neither poses, nor supposes, nor presupposes anything. But it bespeaks all that there is. Its saying arises "without a why."[136]

Analogy requires a First as its support. It institutes God as the supreme support of totality, the foundation both of being and of knowing. The Roman Pantocrator holds in his hand the globe of the universe: in the hand of God all things are, and are explicable. Supreme science is the science 'by the causes.' Being, as the cause of beings, procures their necessary and sufficient condition of possibility.

Under the "without a why" of releasement this foundation gives way. The ground of things is then abyss, nothingness. The analogy of attribution speaks of nothingness as nothingness of essence: the creature is nothing in itself. We shall have to see how nothingness must be thought of if the origin is event, word, self-appropriation.[137]

Notes

1   [The course was not carried out exactly as Schürmann had planned. For example, he never ended up discussing Nicholas of Cusa's speculative mysticism.]

2   [In the margin, Schürmann typed "ch. 13–18." On the basis of the content of what follows in Schürmann's introduction, it appears that he is referring to the chapter divisions of volume 1 of the English translation of Johannes Hirschberger, *Geschichte der Philosophie*, 2 vols. (Freiburg: Herder, 1949–1952); *The History of Philosophy*, 2 vols., trans. Rt. Rev. Anthony N. Fuerst (Milwaukee: Bruce, 1958–1959). Schürmann continues to reference this text under the name "Hirsch" in the margins of his lecture course, although the pagination he provides corresponds neither with the German original nor with the English translation.]

3   [This appears to be Schürmann's translation of the secular cleric Thomas of Ireland's *De tribus sensibus sacrae scripturae*. For another translation, a citation of one of the manuscript sources, and a reference to the original Latin, see Édouard Jeauneau, "Thomas of Ireland and his *De tribus sensibus sacrae scripturae*," in *With Reverence for the Word: Medieval Scriptural Exegesis in Judaism, Christianity, and Islam*, ed. Jane Dammen McAuliffe, Barry D. Walfish, and Joseph W. Goering (Oxford: Oxford University Press, 2003), pp. 288 and 290n22.]

4   [Boethius actually had access to other Aristotelian works, and he also translated the remaining texts of Aristotle's *Organon*, with the exception of the *Posterior Analytics*. However, it is true that until the twelfth century only the *Categories* and *On Interpretation* were widely available. See Bernard G. Dod, "Aristoteles Latinus," in *The Cambridge History of Later Medieval Philosophy: From the Rediscovery of Aristotle to the Disintegration of Scholasticism 1100–1600*, ed. Norman Kretzmann et al. (Cambridge: Cambridge University Press, 1982), pp. 46, 74–75.]

5   [The original Latin can be found in Albert's *Commentarii in II Sententiarum*, dist. 13, C, art. 2, ad object. 1–5, in *B. Alberti Magni Opera Omnia* (Paris, 1890–1899), vol. 27, p. 247.]

6   [In the margin, Schürmann refers to "Hirsch 426" and "ibid. 432." Cf. Hirschberger, *The History of Philosophy*, vol. 1, pp. 394–99.]

7   [See Ulrich von Strassburg, *De Summo Bono* (Hamburg: F. Meiner, 1987–2008), vol. 4, tract. 3, ch. 9, section 9 (p. 142).]

8   [The original Latin can be found in *Metaphysica*, lib. 1, tract. 5, ch. 15, in *B. Alberti Magni Opera Omnia*, vol. 6, p. 113.]

9   [See *De causis et processu universitatis, Liber primus*, tract. 4, ch. 5, in *B. Alberti Magni Opera Omnia*, vol. 10, p. 419.]

10   [See endnote 1, above.]

11   [See, for example, Schürmann's lecture courses on neo-Platonism, medieval concepts of being, and Aristotelian and neo-Platonic elements in late medieval philosophy.]

12   [In the margin Schürmann refers to Gangolf Schrimpf, "Die Synthese des Thomas: Eine Variation des im 9. Jahrhundert grundgelegten mittelalterlichen

Philosophiebegriffs," in *Thomas von Aquin im philosophischen Gespräch*, ed. Wolfgang Kluxen (Freiburg: Alber, 1975), pp. 257–61.]

13 [In the margin Schürmann typed "Hirsch 400." Cf. Hirschberger, *The History of Philosophy*, vol. 1, p. 357.]

14 [Schürmann typed in the margin: " < ill. > d 206–9." Given the references below, this should likely be "Slad."]

15 [I.e., Thomas Aquinas, *Summa theologiae*, First Part, Question 3, Article 4, Reply to Objection 2.]

16 [St. Thomas Aquinas, *Truth*, 3 vols. trans. respectively Robert W. Mulligan, James V. McGlynn, and Robert W. Schmidt (Chicago: Henry Regnery, 1952–1954).]

17 [For translations not available in Pegis, I draw (with modifications) on the translation of the *Summa theologiae* by Laurence Shapcote (Lander, WY: The Aquinas Institute for the Study of Sacred Doctrine, 2012).]

18 [In the margin, Schürmann wrote: "Slad 192ff."]

19 [Pegis p. 124 has: "… and diverse things in idea."]

20 [Schürmann previously had "positedness."]

21 [Here and in many instances below, Schürmann previously had "real" instead of "actual."]

22 [Thomas Aquinas, *Commentary on the Metaphysics*, trans. John P. Rowan (Chicago: H. Regnery, 1961).]

23 [In the margin, Schürmann refers to Volume 1, Column 134 of the *Historisches Wörterbuch der Philosophie*, ed. Joachim Ritter (Basel: Schwabe, 1972).]

24 [Schürmann wrote "Slad 199" in the margin.]

25 [Schürmann wrote "Slad 523 ff" in the margin.]

26 [In the margin Schürmann refers to Ia 29, 1, ad 4 / 39, 2, ad 3.]

27 [Schürmann drew brackets around "to do justice to the chief injunction of the Jewish God: 'Do not confuse me with the universe.'"]

28 [In the margin, Schürmann refers to his *Maître Eckhart ou la joie errante: Sermons allemands traduits et commentés* (Paris: Éditions Planéte, 1972); in English as *Wandering Joy: Meister Eckhart's Mystical Philosophy* (Great Barrington, MA: Lindisfarne Books, 2001). See pp. 170–73 of the latter.]

29 *Metaphysics*, IV 2, 1003 a 33–34; W. D. Ross translates very loosely: "There are many senses in which a thing may be said to 'be,' but all that 'is' is related to one central point, one definite kind of thing, and is not said to 'be' by a mere ambiguity." *The Basic Works of Aristotle*, ed. Richard McKeon (New York: Random House, 1941), p. 732.

30 *Metaphysics*, VII, 1; 1028 a 31: the substance is called *to prōton on*, "the first being"; W. D. Ross translates the entire sentence: "There are several senses in which a thing is said to be first; yet substance is first in every sense" (ibid., p. 783).

31 *Treatise on the Soul*, I, c. 1; 402 b 8. J. A. Smith translates: "the 'universal' being treated either as nothing at all or as a later product," and he explains in a footnote: "i.e., as presupposing the various sorts instead of being presupposed by them" (ibid., p. 536). Neither the translation nor the note show that the universal is here the concept that "follows from" an operation of the mind upon the thing, to the exclusion of a preexisting first being.

32 *Commentary on the First Book of Sentences*, dist. XIX, q. 5, art. 2, ad 1.

33 "Knowledge is predicated neither univocally nor yet purely equivocally of God's knowledge and ours. Instead, it is predicated analogically, or, in other words, according to a proportion." Aquinas, *Truth*, vol. 1, p. 112 f.

34 *Part One*, q. 13, art. 5; trans. Thomas Gilby (New York: McGraw-Hill, 1964), p. 207 f.

35 [Schürmann typed "JdF 113" in the margin.]

36 [Schürmann typed "JdF 130s" in the margin.]

37 [In the margin, Schürmann refers to Jorge Rivera, *Konnaturales Erkennen und vorstellendes Denken* (Freiburg: Karl Alber, 1967), pp. 23–26.]

38 [In the margin, Schürmann refers to Rivera, *Konnaturales Erkennen und vorstellendes Denken*, pp. 28–32.]

39 [Pegis p. 6: "It seems that sacred doctrine is not one science, for according to the Philosopher *that science is one which treats only of one class of subjects.*"]

40 [In the margin, Schürmann refers to column 650 of the entry on "Erkennen, Erkenntnis" ('knowing, knowledge') in Volume 2 of the *Historisches Wörterbuch der Philosophie*, ed. Joachim Ritter (Basel: Schwabe, 1972). The entry continues onto column 651.]

41 [In the typescript Schürmann does not distinguish whether this is the objection or reply. The Latin should read: *Cognitio media est inter cognoscentem et obiectum.* Perhaps Schürmann is quoting from Ludwig Schütz, *Thomas-Lexikon: Sammlung, Übersetzung und Erklärung der in sämtlichen Werken des h. Thomas von Aquin vorkommenden Kunstausdrücke und wissenschaftlichen Aussprüche*, 2nd ed. (Paderborn: Ferdinand Schöningh, 1895), p. 124, which has *Cognitio est media* etc.]

42 [Saint Thomas Aquinas, *Summa Contra Gentiles*, Book One: God, trans. Anton C. Pegis; Book Two: Creation, trans. James F. Anderson (Notre Dame, IN: University of Notre Dame Press, 1956).]

43 [Cf. Rahner, *Spirit in the World*, 77 et passim. Dych renders the latter as "being-present-to-self."]

44 [In the margin, Schürmann refers to Rivera, *Konnaturales Erkennen und vorstellendes Denken*, p. 33.]

45 [In the margin, Schürmann refers to column 1029 of the entry on "Connaturalitas, Erkenntnis durch" ('connaturality, knowledge through') in Volume 1 of the *Historisches Wörterbuch der Philosophie*.]

46 [With the German, Schürmann is referring to a poem by Goethe in his 1810 *Theory of Colours*: "Wär nicht das Auge sonnenhaft, / Die Sonne könnt es nie erblicken; / Läg nicht in uns des Gottes eigne Kraft, / Wie könnt uns Göttliches entzücken?" "Something like the sun the eye must be, / Else it no glint of sun could ever see; / Surely God's own powers with us unite, / Else godly things would not compel delight." Goethe, *The Collected Works*, vol. 1 (*Selected Poems*), ed. Christopher Middleton (Princeton, NJ: Princeton University Press, 1983), pp. 178–79.]

47 [Schürmann typed "JdF 335–8" in the margin.]

48 [In the margin, Schürmann refers to Rivera, *Konnaturales Erkennen und vorstellendes Denken*, pp. 34–39.]

49 [In the margin, Schürmann refers to Rivera, *Konnaturales Erkennen und vorstellendes Denken*, p. 92.]

50 [Sc., of the *Summa Theologiae*. In the margin, Schürmann refers to Rivera, *Konnaturales Erkennen und vorstellendes Denken*, p. 137 f.]

51 [The translation here is Schürmann's modification of J. A. Smith's rendering.]

52 [In the margin, Schürmann refers to Rivera, *Konnaturales Erkennen und vorstellendes Denken*, pp. 139 ff.]

53 [Rahner, *Spirit in the World*, Part Two, Chapter Four: "Conversion to the Phantasm."]

54 [More recent studies date Ockham's life as c. 1287–1347.]

55 [For the source (Trithemius, *De scriptoribus ecclesiasticis*) and status of this report, see C. K. Brampton, "Ockham, Bonagratia and the Emperor Lewis IV," *Medium Ævum* 31, no. 2 (1962): pp. 81–87.]

56 [In the margin Schürmann typed "Hirsch I 562." Cf. Hirschberger, *The History of Philosophy*, vol. 1, p. 475.]

57 [Schürmann cites Philotheus Boehner's translation in Ockham, *Philosophical Writings* (Edinburgh: Bobbs-Merrill, 1964), p. 32, omitting, however, after "but": "is sometimes, indeed always." He continues to modify Boehner's translation without comment in what follows.]

58 [This and the previous two sentences are crossed out.]

59 [Schürmann typed in the margin "Hirsch 563." Cf. Hirschberger, *The History of Philosophy*, vol. 1, p. 476.]

60 [In the margin, Schürmann refers to Erich Hochstetter, *Studien zur Metaphysik und Erkenntnislehre Wilhelms von Ockham* (Berlin: Walter de Gruyter, 1927), p. 24.]

61 ['Singulars' is Schürmann's emendation of the crossed-out word 'particulars.' In *Broken Hegemonies* he explains the difference between these terms as follows: "A fantasm is hegemonic when an entire culture relies on it as if it provided that in the name of which one speaks and acts. Such a chief-represented (*hêgemôn*) is at work upon the unspeakable singular when it calls it a part of the whole; hegemonies transform the singular into a particular. They serve to say what is, to classify and inscribe, to distribute proper and common nouns. Since Plato, making such discriminations has amounted to obliterating the singular for the sake of the common… " Reiner Schürmann, *Broken Hegemonies*, trans. Reginald Lilly (Bloomington: Indiana University Press, 2003), p. 7.]

62 [Schürmann typed a reference in the margin that is partially blotted out. It appears to be "S???lz 100." Perhaps he is referring to Richard Scholz, who published on Ockham's political writings.]

63 [In the margin, Schürmann refers to Hochstetter, *Studien zur Metaphysik und Erkenntnislehre Wilhelms von Ockham*, p. 12 f.]

64 [It would seem that this should read 'negative,' or that the clause should refer to the next sentence.]

65 ['Singular' is Schürmann's emendation of the crossed-out word 'particular.']

66 [In the margin, Schürmann refers to Pierre Alféri, *Guillaume d'Ockham. Le singulier* (Paris: Éditions de Minuit, 1989), pp. 94-98.]

67 [Schürmann refers to Alféri, *Guillaume d'Ockham*, pp. 107–114 in the margin.]

68 [See Joseph C. Wey's edition of Ockham's *Quodlibeta septem*, *Opera theologica*, vol. IX (St. Bonaventure, NY: St. Bonaventure University, 1980), p. 586.]

69 [Schürmann refers to Alféri, *Guillaume d'Ockham*, pp. 119–34 in the margin.]

70 [*Ordo Praedicatorum* (Order of Preachers), i.e. Dominicans.]

71 ['DW' refers to the German works (*Deutsche Werke*) of Meister Eckhart, *Die deutschen und lateinischen Werke*, herausgegeben im Auftrag der deutschen Forschungsgemeinschaft (Stuttgart/Berlin: Kohlhammer, 1936–). 'LW' will refer to the Latin works (*Lateinische Werke*).]

72 Angelus Silesius, physician and poet, who died in 1674, was one of those who no doubt have best understood the Eckhartian preaching on detachment. In his *Cherubinic Pilgrim* he adopts even the vocabulary of the Master. He is, so to speak, Meister Eckhart's versifier. *Abgeschiedenheit, Lauterkeit, Eigenschaft, Bildlosigkeit, Jungfrauschaft* [detachment, purity, property, imagelessness, virginity]—all the Eckhartian terms are known to him: "Weil Abgeschiedenheit sich neimand macht gemein / So muss sie ohne Sucht und eine Jungfrau sein. / Vollkommne Lauterkeit is bild-, forrn-, leiblos, / steht aller Eigenschaft wie Gottens Wesen bloss." "Since detachment makes itself familiar to no one / it has to be without desire and virginal. / Perfect exemption has neither figure, nor form, nor love, / it is devoid of all property, as the being of God." Angelus Silesius, *Der Cherubinische Wandersmann*, ed. Julius Schwabe (Basel: Schwabe, 1955), p. 41.

73 *Alle crêatûren sint ein lûter niht.* Sermon "Omne datum optimum," DW I, pp. 69, 8–70, 1. Cf. also article 26 of the bull which literally repeats this sentence; cf. RS II 4, art. 15 (Gabriel Théry, "Editions critique des pièces relatives au procès d'Eckhart contenues dans le manuscrit 33 b de la bibliothèque de Soest," in *Archives d'histoire doctrinale et littéraire du Moyen Age* I (1926–27): p. 184); and Franz Pelster, "Ein Gutachten aus dem Eckehart-Prozess in Avignon," in *Aus der Geisteswelt des Mittelalters. Festgabe Martin Grabmann* (Münster: Aschendorff 1935), p. 1112.

74 *Alle crêatûren hânt kein wesen, wan ihr wesen swebet an der gegenwerticheit gotes.* Sermon "Omne datum optimum," DW I, p. 70, 2–4.

75 *… Würket diu sêle in unwesene und volget gote, der in unwesene würket.* Sermon "Quasi stella matutina," DW I, p. 151, 11f.

76 *Die Seiendheit des Seienden [wird, R.S.] als die Anwesenheit für das sicherstellende Vorstellen gedacht, Seiendheit ist jetzt Gegenständlichkeit.* Martin Heidegger, *Vorträge und Aufsätze* (Pfullingen: Neske, 1954), p. 74f.; cf. also ibid., p. 240. J. Stambaugh translates: "The beingness of beings is thought as presence for the guarantee of representation. Beingness is now objectivity." Martin Heidegger, *The End of Philosophy*, trans. Joan Stambaugh (New York: Harper & Row, 1973), p. 88.

77 In the mystical German poetry of the thirteenth and fourteenth centuries, we sometimes meet with a play on the oppositions between *iht* and *niht.* Mechthild of Magdeburg writes: "Du solt minnen das niht, / Du solt vliehen das iht… " "Thou shalt love nothing, / Thou shalt flee everything… " Quoted by G. Lüers, *Die Sprache der deutschen Mystik des Mittelalters im Werke der Mechthild von Magdeburg* (Munich: E. Reinhardt, 1926), p. 293. Angelus Silesius writes: "Mensch, sprichst du, dass dich Ichts von Gottes Lieb abhält, / So brauchst du noch nicht recht, wie sich's gehührt der Welt." "Can you say that something

holds you back from the love of God? / You do not yet use the world correctly and as you ought." Silesius, *Der Cherubinische Wandersmann*, p. 39.

78   Sermon "Iusti vivent in aeternum," DW I, p. 106, 1–3: *Gotes sîn mîn sîn und gotes isticheit mîn isticheit.*

79   "Von der übervart der gotheit," in Franz Pfeiffer, *Deutsche Mystiker des vierzehnten Jahrhunderts*, vol. 2, Meister Eckhart, *Predigten und Traktate* (Leipzig: Göschen, 1857), p. 503, 15–17. [Henceforth 'Pf.'] The authenticity of this text is not certain.

80   Sermon "Unus deus et pater omnium," DW I, p. 358, 2: *Uzer gote enist niht dan niht aleine.*

81   E.g., the sermon "Et ecce, homo erat in Ierusalem," Pf. p. 85, 15–17.

82   Sermon "Ave, gratia plena," DW I, p. 376, 7f.

83   Sermon "Quasi stella matutina," DW I, p. 156, 7–9. "Die Schöpfung ist ein Buch, wer's weislich lesen kann, / Dem wird darin gar fein der Schöpfer kundgetan." "Creation is a book: who knows how to read it wisely, / will find the Creator subtly revealed in it." Silesius, *Der Cherubinische Wandersmann*, p. 63.

84   Gabriel Théry, "Le 'Benedictus Deus' de Maître Eckhart," in *Mélanges Joseph de Ghellink* (Gembloux: Duculot, 1951), p. 927.

85   Sermon "Impletum est tempus Elisabeth," DW I, p. 180, 7–13.

86   *Expositio libri Exodi*, n. 117; LW II, p. 112, 7–12.

87   Sermon "Quasi vas auri solidum," DW I, p. 269, 2–7.

88   Ibid., p. 271, 1–3.

89   *Lauffet allein zu der ersten lauterkeyt.* Sermon "Haec dicit dominus: Honora patrem tuum," DW II, p. 475, 3–4. "Wer Gott will gleiche sein, muss allem ungleich werden, / Muss ledig seiner selbst, und bloss sein von Beschwerden." "He who wishes to be like God has to become unlike everything, / He has to be void of himself, and delivered from all pains." Silesius, *Der Cherubinische Wandersmann*, p. 74.

90   Sermon "Quasi stella matutina," DW I, p. 154, 1–3.

91   Sermon "Quasi vas auri solidum," DW I, pp. 265, 9–269, 1.

92   Sermon "Iusti vivent in aeternum," DW I, p. 106, 4–107, 4.

93   Sermon "Vidi supra montem Syon," DW I, pp. 215, 10–216, 7.

94   Sermon "Et ecce, homo erat in Ierusalem," Pf. p. 86, 11.

95   Sermon "Quis puer iste erit?" Pf. p. 196, 40f.

96   Fire *Suochet in ime daz eine*; Pf. p. 431, 19–34. Angelus Silesius summarizes this development in two lines: "Gott ist in mir das Feu'r, und ich in ihm der Schein: / Sind wir einander nicht ganz inniglich gemein?" "God in me is the fire, I am in him the clarity: / Are we not very closely united?" Silesius, *Der Cherubinische Wandersmann*, p. 20.

97   Sermon "Iusti vivent in aeternum," DW I, p. 111, 7. The inquisitors translate *ein unglîch* by *unum, non simile:* RS 11,4 art. I (Théry, "Editions critique des pièces relatives au procès d'Eckhart," p. 177), a wording repeated by the bull, art. 10, in Heinrich Denzinger and Adolf Schönmetzer, *Enchiridion Symbolorum, Definitionum et Declarationum de rebus fidei et morum* (Freiburg: Herder, 1963), n. 960: *sic ergo convertor in eum, quod ipse operatur me suum esse unum, non simile.* Expressions like *niht glîch, das selbe,* 'not alike, but the same,' are frequent:

Pf. 85, 26f., with regard to the relationship between Father and Son; Pf. 151, 19 with regard to God in himself and God who is born in the mind; Pf. 163, 33–38, with regard to God and the mind.

98 *Daz würken und daz werden ist ein... Got und ich wir sint ein in disem gewürke; er würket und ich gewirde...* Sermon "Iusti vivent in aeternum," DW I, pp. 114, 2–115, 2.

99 Sermon "Convescens praecepit eis," DW II, pp. 88, 3–89, 3.

100 *Niht în geslozzen, niht vereiniget, mêr: ez ist ein.* Sermon "Et ecce, homo erat in Ierusalem," Pf. pp. 85, 36–86, 4.

101 *Er gebirt mich sich und sich mich und mich sîn wesen und sîn natûre... Dâ ist ein leben und ein wesen und ein werk.* Sermon "Iusti vivent in aeternum," DW I, p. 109, 9–1l.

102 *Der grunt gotes unde der grunt der sêle sint ein wesen.* Treatise "Daz ist swester Katrei," Pf. p. 467, 15. Authenticity of this text is not universally recognized.

103 Sermon "Ave, gratia plena," DW I, p. 381, 1. Angelus Silesius literally repeats this expression: "In Gott wird nichts erkannt; er ist ein einig Ein, / Was man in ihm erkennt, das muss man selber sein." "Nothing is known in God, he is a unique One, / that which is known of him, one must be oneself." Silesius, *Der Cherubinische Wandersmann*, p. 35.

104 Sermon "Qui audit me," DW I, p. 199, 1–6.

105 *Swaz in gote ist, daz ist got.* Sermon "Nunc scio vere," DW I, p. 56, 8; the censors of the Inquisition translated: *Omne quod est, hoc est deus* [Everything that is is in God]! RS II, art. 50 (Théry, "Editions critique des pièces relatives au procès d'Eckhart," p. 252). The sentence *Quidquid in Deo est, Deus est* was the solemn formulation by which the Synod of Reims in 1148 refuted the real distinction in God, a theory attributed to Gilbert de Poitiers; Joannes Dominicus Mansi, *Sacrorum Conciliorum nova et amplissima collectio* (Paris-Leipzig, 1901–1927), vol. 21, col. 726E. [Schürmann refers to Sermon "Nolite timere eos," Pf. p. 18, 15.] This erroneous translation of the statements of Meister Eckhart is partly based on the accusation of pantheism. Angelus Silesius writes: "Ich muss ein Schein im Schein, / Ich muss ein Wort im Wort, ein Gott in Gotte sein." "I have to be clarity in clarity, / I have to be a Word in the Word, God in God." "In Gott ist alles Gott: ein einz'ges Würmelein / Das ist in Gott so viel als tausend Gotte sein." "In God everything is God: the least little worm / Is no less in God than are a thousand gods." Silesius, *Der Cherubinische Wandersmann*, pp. 19, 132.

106 "Dies alles ist ein Spiel, das sich die Gottheit macht, / Sie hat die Kreatur um ihretwilln erdacht." "All this is a play that the Godhead gives itself / It has conceived the creature for its own sake." Silesius, *Der Cherubinische Wandersmann*, p. 45.

107 [At the bottom of the page, Schürmann quotes from his translation of Eckhart's sermon "Like a Vase of Massive Gold": "I wondered recently if I should accept or desire anything from God. I shall consider this carefully, for if I accepted something from God, I would be inferior to God like a serf, and he, in giving, would be like a lord. But such should not be our relation." Schürmann, *Wandering Joy*, 107.]

108 Sermon "Qui audit me," DW I, p. 199, 9–11.

109 Sermon "Mulier, venit hora." [Schürmann refers to his translation of the sermon in *Wandering Joy*, chapter 2; see p. 54 for the passage.]

110 Sermon "Omne datum optimum," DW I, p. 69, 2–4.

111 Sermon "In diebus suis," DW I, p. 171, 12–15. "Wo ist mein Aufenthalt? Wo ich und du nicht stehen. / Wo ist mein letztes End, in welches ich soll gehen? / Da wo man keines findt. Wo soll ich dann nun hin? / Ich muss noch über Gott in eine Wüste ziehn." "Where shall I stay? Where you and I are not. / Where is the last end to which I should tend? / Where one finds none. Where then shall I go? / I must move still higher than God, into a desert." Silesius, *Der Cherubinische Wandersmann*, p. 61.

112 Sermon "Nolite timere eos," Pf. p. 181, 1–10.

113 Sermon "Beati pauperes spiritu," DW II, p. 492, 3–4; 7–9.

114 Ibid., DW II, pp. 205, 6–504, 3; Angelus Silesius writes: "Dass Gott so selig ist und lebet ohn Verlangen, / Hat er sowohl von mir, als ich von ihm empfangen." "That God be happy and live without desire / He has received from me as much as I from him." Silesius, *Der Cherubinische Wandersmann*, p. 20.

115 Shizuteru Ueda, "Über den Sprachgebrauch Meister Eckharts," in *Glaube, Geist, Geschichte. Festschrift für Ernst Benz* (Leiden: Brill, 1967), pp. 266f. Ueda analyzes the texts in which this expression occurs.

116 ... *Sîn nâtûre twinget in dar zuo.* Sermon "Dilectus deo et hominibus," Pf. p. 231, 13–16.

117 "Commentary on the Book of Exodus," n. 16, LW II, p. 22, 3–6. With these lines Meister Eckhart comments on the verse of John: *in ipso vita erat* [in him was life] (John 1:4). On the history of the translation "what has been created was life in him," cf. Vladimir Lossky, *Théologie négative et connaissance de Dieu chez Maître Eckhart* (Paris: Vrin, 1960), p. 115n65. The equivalence between 'life' and 'boiling' or 'seething' goes back to an old Greek etymology according to which *zēn*, to live, would derive from *zeein*, to boil, to seethe. This connection is attested, e.g., in Plotinus, *The Enneads* VI, 7,12: "There no indigence or impotence can exist but all must be teeming, seething, with life," trans. Stephen McKenna, 4th ed., rev. B. S. Page (New York: Faber and Faber, 1969), p. 570. Angelus Silesius takes up this teaching: "Gott gleich sich einem Brunn, er fleusst ganz mildiglich / Heraus in sein Geschöpf und bleibet doch in sich." "God is like a fountain, he generously runs off / Into his creature, and still remains in himself." "Eh ich etwas ward, da war ich Gottes Leben, / Drum hat er auch für mich sich ganz und gar ergeben." "Before I became one thing, I was the life of God, / That is why he gave himself entirely up for me." Silesius, *Der Cherubinische Wandersmann*, pp. 68, 72. The author indicates in a note that he is referring to John 1:4; Silesius should therefore be added to Lossky's list of names.

118 Sermon "In hoc apparuit," DW I, p. 94, 4f.

119 Ibid., p. 95, 1–3.

120 Sermon "Homo quidam nobilis," DW I, p. 246, 10.

121 Sermon "Stetit Jesus in media," DW II, p. 190, 1–2.

122 Cf. my article on releasement in Meister Eckhart, Heidegger, and Suzuki, with an explanation of the "Ten cowherding pictures": "Trois penseurs du délaissement," in *The Journal of the History of Philosophy* 12, no. 4 (October 1974): pp. 455–78 and 13, no. 1 (January 1975): pp. 43–60.

123 Sermon "In hoc apparuit," DW I, p. 91, 3–7.

124 "General Prologue" to the *Opus Tripartitum,* LW I, p. 156. A. Maurer translates: "Existence is God," in Master Eckhart, *Parisian Questions and Prologues,* p. 77, but *esse* refers to the act of being, not to existence as opposed to essence. See also the sermon "Woman, the Hour Is Coming." [Schürmann refers to his commentary on the sermon in *Wandering Joy,* 62–65.]

125 Étienne Gilson, *History of Christian Philosophy in the Middle Ages* (New York: Random House, 1955), p. 441: "Being is, so to speak, imputed to beings by God without ever becoming their own being, about in the same way as in Luther's theology justice will be imputed to the just without ever becoming their own justice."

126 *Book of the Divine Consolation,* DW V, p. 37, 5. Cf. also the end of the sermon "Proclaim the Word." [Schürmann refers to pages of his translation of the sermon in *Wandering Joy,* 181–82.]

127 *Commentary on the Book of Ecclesiasticus,* n. 52; LW II, pp. 280f.

128 Josef Koch, in "Zur Analogielehre Meister Eckharts," in *Mélanges offerts à Étienne Gilson* (Toronto: Pontifical Institute of Mediaeval Studies; Paris: J. Vrin, 1959), pp. 347–350, has shown that this doctrine can call upon antecedents such as Otto of Freising, Gilbert of Porrée, and Augustine.

129 "All the just are so by justice which is one in number; that is, a number without number and one without one; or rather: a oneness above oneness by which all the just, inasmuch as they are just, are one." *Commentary on the Book of Wisdom,* n. 44; LW II, p. 366, 4–7.

130 [For Schürmann's translation of this sermon see Schürmann, *Wandering Joy,* 129–34.]

131 Sermon "Et ecce, homo erat in Ierusalem," Pf. p. 88, 8.

132 Sermon "Laudate caeli," Pf. p. 300, 7–11.

133 *Parisian Questions,* question I, n. 6 and 8; LW V, pp. 42, 7–45, 5. English translation slightly modified from Master Eckhart, *Parisian Questions and Prologues,* pp. 46–48.

134 Sermon "Praedica verbum." [Schürmann refers to his translation of this passage in *Wandering Joy,* p. 179.]

135 Sermon "Beati pauperes." [Schürmann refers to his translation of this passage in *Wandering Joy,* p. 215.]

136 Sermon "In hoc apparuit," DW I, p. 90, 12.

137 [The course breaks off here. For more see Schürmann, *Wandering Joy,* 187 ff.]

Afterword

Ian Alexander Moore

In his posthumously published magnum opus, *Broken Hegemonies*, Reiner Schürmann suggests that the medieval Scotists, in particular William of Ockham, offer an alternative to the "hegemonic fantasm" of nature that reigned in the Latinate West from the time of Cicero and Augustine until the advent of self-consciousness in the modern vernacular of Luther.[1] For those familiar with Schürmann's earlier books, this should come as a surprise. Not only is Ockham not mentioned there, but Scotus himself comes in for harsh treatment.[2] Since Schürmann does not develop his later contention in *Broken Hegemonies*, instead electing and analyzing Meister Eckhart as a better representative for the destitution of the epochal principle of nature,[3] one is left to wonder whether and how the Scotists really fit into Schürmann's project.

Fortunately, in the present volume, Schürmann shows how "natural order become[s] dispersed" on account of Ockham's conceptualism (p. 77). By emphasizing the absolute power of God and the priority of singulars, and adhering only to the principle of non-contradiction as universal, Ockham's philosophy "suffices to dethrone teleology from the rank of ultimacy that it held since classical Greece," and thus "truly goes beyond the boundaries of medieval thought" (p. 78-79). Little wonder, then, that in one of his outlines for Part II of *Broken Hegemonies*, Schürmann had planned

---

1   Reiner Schürmann, *Des hégémonies brisées* (Zurich-Berlin: DIAPHANES, 2017), pp. 240-41, 246, 323, 347, 354, 392, 706; *Broken Hegemonies*, trans. Reginald Lilly (Bloomington: Indiana University Press, 2003), pp. 200, 202, 252, 271-72, 291, 298, 332, 614.

2   Reiner Schürmann, *Le principe d'anarchie: Heidegger et la question de l'agir* (Bienne-Paris: DIAPHANES, 2013), pp. 148-57; *Heidegger on Being and Acting: From Principles to Anarchy*, trans. Christine-Marie Gros in collaboration with the author (Bloomington: Indiana University Press, 1990), pp. 107-112.

3   Schürmann, *Des hégémonies brisées*, Deuxième Partie, Section II (esp. pp. 324-25); *Broken Hegemonies*, Part Two, Section II (esp. pp. 272-73).

on writing precisely on Scotus and Ockham. Although, as he noted in the outline, this material was "not yet written," and although it would never be written as such, we may reasonably assume that the section on Ockham in the present volume would have served as its basis.[4] It is all the more remarkable that this section (or at least parts of it) dates from 1978, fifteen years before Schürmann's untimely death and the completion of his masterwork.

This volume does not just offer a novel and singular treatment of Ockham, though. It also situates Ockham's work within the context of a broader movement of the High Middle Ages, namely, what Schürmann identifies as 'neo-Aristotelianism' (which is not, of course, to be confused with the twentieth-century method of rhetorical criticism that goes by the same name). Schürmann argues that, in between the spiritual Carolingian Renaissance of the ninth century and the secular Humanist Renaissance of the fifteenth and sixteenth centuries, there was a Medieval Renaissance connected with the revival of Roman law in the twelfth century and the rediscovery of Aristotle in the thirteenth. With the decline of feudal hierarchy and the rise of relatively autonomous centers of learning, the representatives of the Medieval Renaissance placed greater emphasis on the autonomy of reason and the independent intelligibility of the physical world. Even though Aristotle, for his part, became a new sort of authority in this transition, and even though the 'neo-' in 'neo-Aristotelianism' by no means signifies a shift on the order of neo-Platonism, figures such as Thomas Aquinas, Ockham, and Eckhart took Aristotle in directions the ancient Greek philosopher never could have imagined. These three medieval philosophers were guided in this endeavor by Albert the Great, who (1) challenged the older monist ontology with his distinction between the being of the first creative intelligence and that of the Aristotelian active intellect or God, (2) his destruction of the identity between the logical and real orders of universals, and (3) his affirmation of the substantiality of the soul. After briefly discussing these three contributions by Albert in the introduction, Schürmann

---

4   My thanks to Francesco Guercio for this information.

uses them as orientation for interpreting Aquinas, Ockham, and Eckhart, respectively, in the remainder of the volume.

Parts I and II are devoted to Aquinas, whose work Schürmann interprets as, in effect, a tunnel under the unstable cathedral of Latin metaphysics: although Aquinas may have dug it in order to erect support beams, he thereby made way for the bombs that Ockham and Eckhart would build from this edifice's own materials and detonate in his wake.

The first part provides an at once detailed and synoptic treatment of the various senses of 'being' in Aquinas' work. On the one hand, Aquinas supports the tradition he inherits with his doctrine of the 'analogy of being.' He expands Aristotle's distinction between potency and actuality *in* substances to apply *to* substances, which themselves become potential with respect to an infinite, purely actual 'act of being' that grounds and inheres in everything that is. This inherence does not lead to pantheism or ontological monism, however, since, according to Aquinas' unique development of Aristotelian analogy, beings (creatures) are still related to the highest being (to God the creator) in the mode of deficient similitude; they are 'lesser in being.' Hierarchy still reigns.

On the other hand, even though everything is accordingly dependent on God, Aquinas' approach allows for a certain autonomy of creatures. They are like wood set aflame: once the log catches fire, it can burn all on its own; once creatures receive the act from God, they are able, of themselves, to deploy it to unfold what they, in each case, are. The act thus "preserves the plurality of individuals" (p. 50) and justifies, from a theological perspective, Aquinas' great interest in them. Indeed, Schürmann notes that "[t]his stress on individuation, which entails ontological autonomy, is what characterizes most deeply the new achievement of philosophy in medieval neo-Aristotelianism" (p. 37). Concomitantly, the vocabulary of act proffers an incipient challenge to rank. The being of creatures will invariably be inferior to the being of God, but the act will remain unchanged. Thus, if we look to the act *alone*, we will be unable to discern any hierarchy in creatures. Aquinas' neo-Aristotelian successors will advance both of these moves taken by Aquinas, namely, the turn toward singularity (especially Ockham) and the critique of hierarchy (especially Eckhart).

Before moving on to Aquinas' successors, Schürmann draws out the epistemological implications of Aquinas' ontology in the second part of the volume. As pure actuality is to finite acts, so, Schürmann explains, is knowledge by 'connaturality'[5] to knowledge of particular things, i.e. to knowledge by 'conformity.' Before I can come to know some particular thing or some state of affairs (that the table is sturdy, say), and thus before I can will something or other (to write on the table), there must be some common ground or nature between the thing (in this case the table) and me, i.e. our identical pure actuality, on which I can establish the relation of factual knowledge or decide in favor of a particular action. At the most basic level, I already have and am had by what I want to know or will to do.

In Part III, Schürmann shows how Ockham develops a powerful alternative to this teaching of knowledge by connaturality. Ockham applies his famous razor to shave off the formal and final causes of knowledge. When I know something, it is not, as on the Aristotelian model, because I have drawn out its essence (formal cause) and derived the concept proper to it (final cause). Rather, it is because I have fabricated a universal in my mind and *imposed* it on the singular thing of my experience. Concepts no longer correspond to essences; they are merely signs concocted by convention, pointing at singulars. Hence, from a strict Aristotelian or Thomist perspective, I don't actually know anything. For there is no shared or communicated being. Everything instead depends on the seemingly constant, yet arbitrary and always changeable activity of God's will. Tomorrow everything could be different; even so-called laws of nature could be violated. Art has outstripped nature. The biblical maker God, who need not work from models, has supplanted his rational counterpart: the God of the philosophers has died.

The death of the rational God is not a complete loss, though, since it actually frees God to do as he will and at the same time saves the life of singulars. Ockham has thus taken "a further step in the recognition of the autonomy of things" (p. 70). But what

---

5   As is the case with Ockham, connaturality appears in *Broken Hegemonies* without receiving extensive treatment. See Schürmann, *Des hégémonies brisées*, pp. 323, 365, 371; *Broken Hegemonies*, pp. 271, 308, 313.

to do in the face of such caprice? Recalling other writings, we can imagine Schürmann's response: accept dispersion, let singulars be in all their singularity, "love the interruptions that mortify [your] natural, native megalomania."[6]

If Ockham cuts off the ontological support for connaturality, Eckhart lets it mature into something subversive by taking it to its extreme conclusion: in my ground I am united with God—nay, the God beyond God, the 'Godhead,' and I are (verbally, processually, before all 'substance metaphysics') a single oneness (*ein einic ein*)—and I know all things. The fourth and final part of the volume examines Eckhart's 'speculative mysticism' (without, as projected in the introduction, additionally addressing that of Nicholas of Cusa[7]). This part derives mostly from the English edition of Schürmann's first book, *Wandering Joy*,[8] but is nevertheless interesting to read in the context of the neo-Aristotelianism of the Medieval Renaissance.

Schürmann traces the quadripartite itinerary of Eckhart's imperative of 'detachment' (*abegescheidenheit*) or 'releasement' (*gelâzenheit*), where the soul moves from the experience of dissimilarity from God, through the recognition of similarity to and identity with God, and finally to the breakthrough beyond God to his abyssal, reasonless ground that is also the soul's ground. Viewed in their emergence from this dark, anarchic source, God, the human being, and the world are all one: "releasement leads beings back to their primitive 'connaturality'" (p. 95). Viewed apart from this source, they are nothing. There are, contra Aquinas, accordingly no grades of being. Even the distinction between creature and creator, on which Ockham relied, breaks down. If Ockham's thought allows us

---

6   Schürmann, *Des hégémonies brisées*, p. 304; *Broken Hegemonies*, p. 254.

7   For a brief but provocative reference to Cusa as a third alternative to the hegemonic fantasm of nature (in addition to Ockham and Eckhart), see Schürmann, *Des hégémonies brisées*, p. 324; *Broken Hegemonies*, p. 272.

8   Reiner Schürmann, *Wandering Joy: Meister Eckhart's Mystical Philosophy* (Great Barrington, MA: Lindisfarne, 2001), pp. 81-95, 101-117, 173-77, 182-87. Originally published in English as *Meister Eckhart: Mystic and Philosopher* (Bloomington: Indiana University Press, 1978). This is a revised and expanded version of *Maître Eckhart ou la joie errante* (Paris: Éditions Planète, 1972); the latter was republished in Paris: Éditions Payot & Rivages, 2005.

to celebrate singulars from the humble perspective of createdness, Eckhart's thought allows us to see that, in our superhuman ground, we are their very origin and can thus let them be; indeed we are even the origin of God, regardless of whether he is conceived primarily in terms of reason (Aquinas) or primarily in terms of will (Ockham). In a powerful passage from *Wandering Joy*, published already in 1972 and included again in this volume, a passage that can be seen as a sort of summa of Schürmann's lifelong interest in anarchy and living 'without why,' we read:

> In its pre-originary origin the will sets itself loose from any principle; it is anarchic. Nothing precedes it; therefore it has nothing to obey, except itself. Detachment, at this stage, ignores or suspends any reference to determinate being. Man is perfectly released. He exists himself as the pre-originary origin, he is the origin of the origin, and no one can lay restrictions upon his freedom, not even God. (100)[9]

***

The present volume is based on Schürmann's lecture course, "Medieval Philosophy II: Neo-Aristotelianism," held at the New School for Social Research in Spring 1978 and then in Spring 1991. To better convey its content and trajectory, I have retitled the material "Neo-Aristotelianism and the Medieval Renaissance: On Aquinas, Ockham, and Eckhart." Abbreviations have been written out in full, and foreign words and titles have been italicized. Spelling and grammatical mistakes have been corrected without comment. With few exceptions, I have not included transcriptions of Schürmann's handwritten marginalia, due either to their illegibility or to lack of substantive interest. When possible, I have filled in Schürmann's elliptical citations of the secondary literature on which he relies. My editorial notes and interpolations have been placed in square brackets. I have marked Schürmann's bracketed interpolations with

---

9   Cf. Schürmann, *Maître Eckhart ou la joie errante* (Éditions Payot & Rivages), p. 197; *Wandering Joy*, p. 117.

the cipher 'RS,' though not when he provides the original language for a quote (which I have never done). Finally, I have provided translations for Schürmann's foreign terms and citations. When relevant, I refer to published English translations, although I have occasionally modified these, without comment, so as to accord with Schürmann's terminology and interpretation.

Tentative Chronology of Reiner Schürmann's Courses at the New School for Social Research

Year	Term	Course Title	All Instances
1975	Summer	*Nietzsche and the Problem of Truth* [The Philosophy of Nietzsche]	1975, Summer 1977, Fall 1984, Spring 1988, Spring
	Fall	*Augustine's Philosophy of Language* [Augustine's Philosophy of Mind]	1975, Fall 1979, Fall 1984, Fall 1991, Fall
		Aristotelian & Neoplatonic Elements in Late Medieval Philosophy [Medieval Neoplatonism and Aristotelianism]	1975, Fall 1981, Spring 1987, Spring
		Karl Jaspers' Philosophy of Existence	1975, Fall 1979, Spring
1976	Spring	*Plotinus –* *A Study of the Enneads with Particular Emphasis on En. IV and VI* [Plotinus—The Philosophy of Plotinus]	1976, Spring 1978, Fall 1983, Fall 1988, Fall 1992, Fall
		The Scope of Hermeneutics [Hermeneutics]	1976, Spring 1979, Fall 1986, Fall
	Fall	*The Contemporary Crisis in the Philosophy of Man* [Philosophical Anthropology II: Its Contemporary Crisis]*	1976, Fall* 1981, Spring 1990, Spring
		*Medieval Philosophy I: Neoplatonism**	1976, Fall* 1979, Spring 1980, Fall (ver. II) 1990, Spring (ver. I)

Year	Term	Course Title	All Instances
1977	Spring	Heidegger's Destruction of Metaphysics* [The Phenomenology of the Later Heidegger]	1977, Spring* 1980, Spring 1984, Fall 1994, Spring †
		Kant's Critique of Pure Reason – Part II*	1977, Spring 1980, Spring 1988, Spring 1988 Fall
	Fall	Reading Marx	1977, Fall
		The Philosophy of Nietzsche [The Philosophy of Nietzsche]	1975, Summer 1977, Fall 1984, Spring 1988, Spring
		Medieval Concepts of Being	1977, Fall 1982, Fall
1978	Spring	Medieval Philosophy II: Neo-Aristotelianism (13th–14th centuries)	1978, Spring; 1991, Spring
		Heidegger as an Interpreter of Kant	1978, Spring 1985, Spring 1991, Spring
	Fall	The Philosophy of Plotinus [Plotinus—The Philosophy of Plotinus]	1976, Spring 1978, Fall 1983, Fall 1988, Fall 1992, Fall
		Contemporary French Philosophy [From Transcendentalism to "Post-Structuralism"; Systems and Breaks: Foucault and Derrida †]	1978, Fall 1983, Spring 1994, Spring †
		Heidegger's Being and Time*	1978, Fall* 1982, Spring 1986, Fall; 1993, Spring

Year	Term	Course Title	All Instances
1979	Spring	*Medieval Philosophy I: Neoplatonism*	<u>1976, Fall*</u> 1979, Spring <u>1980, Fall</u> <u>(ver. II)</u> <u>1990, Spring</u> <u>(ver. I)</u>
		Karl Jaspers' Philosophy of Existence	1975, Fall <u>1979, Spring</u>
		Kant's Practical Philosophy**	1979, Spring**
	Fall	*Augustine's Philosophy of Mind* [Augustine's Philosophy of Language]	1975, Fall 1979, Fall 1984, Fall <u>1991, Fall</u>
		Kant's Critique of Pure Reason – Part I	<u>1979, Fall,</u> <u>1982, Fall</u> 1987, Fall <u>1988, Spring*</u>
		Hermeneutics [The Scope of Hermeneutics]	<u>1976, Spring</u> <u>1979, Fall</u> <u>1986, Fall</u>

Year	Term	Course Title	All Instances
1980	Spring	Kant's Critique of Pure Reason – Part II	1977, Spring* 1980, Spring 1988, Spring 1988, Fall
		The Phenomenology of the Later Heidegger [Heidegger's Destruction of Metaphysics]	1977, Spring 1980, Spring 1984, Fall 1994, Spring †
	Fall	Medieval Philosophy I: Neoplatonism (ver. II)	1976, Fall* 1979, Spring 1980, Fall (ver. II) 1990, Spring (ver. I)
		Modern Philosophies of the Will	1980, Fall 1987, Spring 1992, Spring
		Philosophical Anthropology	1980, Fall 1989, Spring
1981	Spring	Aristotelian & Neoplatonic Elements in Late Medieval Philosophy [Medieval Neoplatonism and Aristotelianism]	1975, Fall 1981, Spring 1987, Spring
		The Contemporary Crisis in the Philosophy of Man [Philosophical Anthropology II: Its Contemporary Crisis]	1976, Fall* 1981, Spring 1990, Spring

Year	Term	Course Title	All Instances
1982	Spring	*Kant's Political Philosophy*	*1982, Spring* *1992, Fall*
		Heidegger's Being and Time	*1978, Fall** *1982, Spring* *1986, Fall* *1993, Spring*
		Seminar in Methodological Problems *[X-listed Econ J323s; co-taught with* *Prof. R. L. Heilbroner]*	*1982, Spring*
	Fall	*Medieval Concepts of Being*	*1977, Fall* *1982, Fall*
		Kant's Critique of Pure Reason – Part I	*1979, Fall,* *1982, Fall* *1987, Fall* *1988, Spring**
1983	Spring	*From Transcendentalism to* *"Post-Structuralism"* *[Contemporary French Philosophy;* *Systems and Breaks: Foucault and Derrida †]*	*1978, Fall* *1983, Spring* *1994, Spring* †
	Fall	*The Philosophy of Plotinus* *[Plotinus – A Study of the Enneads* *with Particular Emphasis on En. IV and VI; Plotinus]*	*1976, Spring* *1978, Fall* *1983, Fall* *1988, Fall* *1992, Fall*
		Kant's Critique of Judgment	*1983, Fall* *1990, Spring*

Year	Term	Course Title	All Instances
1984	Spring	*Medieval Practical Philosophy* [Latin Metaphysics of Nature]	*1984, Spring* *1988, Spring*
		The Philosophy of Nietzsche [Nietzsche and the Problem of Truth]	1975, Summer *1977, Fall* 1984, Spring *1988, Spring*
	Fall	*Augustine's Philosophy of Mind* [Augustine's Philosophy of Language]	1975, Fall 1979, Fall 1984, Fall *1991, Fall*
		Heidegger's Destruction of Metaphysics [The Phenomenology of the Later Heidegger]	1977, Spring* *1980, Spring* 1984, Fall 1994, Spring †
1985	Spring	*Greek and Latin Philosophies of Time*	*1985 Spring* *1989, Spring*
		Heidegger as an Interpreter of Kant	*1978, Spring* 1985, Spring 1991, Spring
1986	Fall	*Hermeneutics* [The Scope of Hermeneutics]	*1976, Spring* *1979, Fall* *1986, Fall*
		Heidegger's Being and Time	*1978, Fall** *1982, Spring* *1986, Fall* *1993, Spring*
		Parmenides	*1986, Fall* *1991, Fall*

Year	Term	Course Title	All Instances
1987	Spring	*Medieval Neoplatonism and Aristotelianism* [Aristotelian & Neoplatonic Elements in Late Medieval Philosophy]	1975, Fall 1981, Spring 1987, Spring
		Modern Philosophies of the Will	1980, Fall 1987, Spring 1992, Spring
	Fall	*Kant's Critique of Pure Reason – Part I*	1979, Fall 1982, Fall 1987, Fall 1988, Spring*
1988	Spring	*Latin Metaphysics of Nature* [Medieval Practical Philosophy]	1984, Spring 1988, Spring
		The Philosophy of Nietzsche [Nietzsche and the Problem of Truth]	1975, Summer 1977, Fall 1984, Spring 1988, Spring
		Kant's Critique of Pure Reason – Part I	1979, Fall, 1982, Fall 1987, Fall 1988, Spring*
		Kant's Critique of Pure Reason – Part II	1977, Spring 1980, Spring 1988, Spring 1988, Fall
	Fall	*Plotinus* [The Philosophy of Plotinus; Plotinus—A Study of the Enneads with Particular Emphasis on En. IV and VI]	1976, Spring 1978, Fall 1983, Fall 1988, Fall 1992, Fall
		Kant's Critique of Pure Reason – Part II	1977, Spring* 1980, Spring 1988, Spring 1988, Fall

Year	Term	Course Title	All Instances
1989	Spring	*Greek and Latin Philosophies of Time*	*1985, Spring* *1989, Spring*
		Philosophical Anthropology: *An Introduction*	*1980, Fall* *1989, Spring*
	Fall	*Heidegger's Thinking in the 30s*	*1989, Fall*
1990	Spring	*Medieval Philosophy I* *(Neoplatonism; version I)*	*1976, Fall** *1979, Spring* *1980, Fall* *(ver. II)* *1990, Spring* *(ver. I)*
		Kant's Critique of Judgment	*1983, Fall* *1990, Spring*
		Seminar on Philosophical Anthropology *II: Its Contemporary Crisis* [The Contemporary Crisis in the Philosophy of Man]	*1976, Fall** *1981, Spring* *1990, Spring*
1991	Spring	*Medieval Philosophy II:* *Neo-Aristotelianism* *(13th–14th centuries)*	*1978, Spring* *1991, Spring*
		Seminar on Heidegger *as an Interpreter of Kant*	*1978, Spring* *1985, Spring* *1991, Spring*
	Fall	*Parmenides*	*1986, Fall* *1991, Fall*
		Augustine's Philosophy of Mind [Augustine's Philosophy of Language]	*1975, Fall* *1979, Fall* *1984, Fall* *1991, Fall*

Year	Term	Course Title	All Instances
1992	Spring	*Luther:* *The Origin of Modern Self-consciousness*	<u>1992, Spring</u>
		Modern Philosophies of the Will	<u>1980, Fall;</u> 1987, Spring <u>1992, Spring</u>
	Fall	*Kant's Political Philosophy*	<u>1982, Spring</u> <u>1992, Fall</u>
		Plotinus [The Philosophy of Plotinus; Plotinus—A Study of the Enneads with Particular Emphasis on En. IV and VI]	1976, Spring 1978, Fall 1983, Fall 1988, Fall <u>1992, Fall</u>
1993	Spring	*Heidegger's Being and Time*	<u>1978, Fall*</u> <u>1982, Spring</u> <u>1986, Fall</u> <u>1993, Spring</u>
		Meister Eckhart	<u>1993, Spring</u>
1994 †	Spring †	*Heidegger's 'Destruction of Metaphysics'* † [The Phenomenology of the Later Heidegger]	1977, Spring* <u>1980, Spring</u> 1984, Fall 1994, Spring †
		Systems and Breaks: *Foucault and Derrida* † [Contemporary French Philosophy; From Transcendentalism to "Post-Structuralism"]	<u>1978, Fall</u> <u>1983, Spring;</u> 1994, Spring †

The *Chronology* is based on the NSSR Bulletin and cross-referenced with the Lecture Notes

— the underlined years/terms—e.g. <u>1980, Spring</u>—are the ones mentioned in the Lecture Notes
— * = Course *is not* mentioned in the NSSR Bulletin although Lecture Notes, with specific years/terms, have been found
— ** = Course *is* mentioned in the NSSR Bulletin but *no* Lecture Notes linked to the former have been found
— [ ] = alternative title for different years/terms
— † = Course *is* mentioned in the NSSR Bulletin but was never taught due to death.

Lecture Notes of Reiner Schürmann at the NSSR— Pierre Adler's Inventory (1994)

Volume I: Ancient Philosophy	Volume II: Medieval Philosophy	Volume III: Early Modern Philosophy
• Parmenides • Greek and Latin Philosophies of Time • The Philosophy of Plotinus • Augustine's Philosophy of Mind • Medieval Practical Philosophy	• Medieval Philosophy I: Neoplatonism • Medieval Philosophy I: Neoplatonism Version II • Medieval Philosophy II: Neo-Aristotelianism (13th/14th centuries) • Medieval Concepts of Being • Aristotelian and Neo-Platonic Elements in Late Medieval Philosophy • Meister Eckhart	• Luther: The Origin of Modern Self-consciousness • Kant's *Critique of Pure Reason* Part I • Kant's *Critique of Pure Reason* Part II • Kant's *Critique of Judgment*

Volume IV: Philosophy in Modernity	Volume V: Heidegger	Volume VI: 20th Century Philosophy
• Kant's Political Philosophy • Reading Marx • The Philosophy of Nietzsche • Modern Philosophies of Will • Karl Jaspers' Philosophy of Existence	• Heidegger's *Being and Time* • Heidegger's Destruction of Metaphysics • Heidegger as an Interpreter of Kant • Heidegger's Thinking in the 1930s	• Hermeneutics • Philosophical Anthropology • Philosophical Anthropology II, Its Contemporary Crisis • Methodology of Social Sciences (co-taught with Prof Heilbroner) • Contemporary French Philosophy

Reiner Schürmann
Selected Writings and Lecture Notes

Edited by
Francesco Guercio, Michael Heitz,
Malte Fabian Rauch, and Nicolas Schneider

This edition aims to provide a broader perspective on the prolific, multifaceted, and still largely unrecognized body of work produced by Reiner Schürmann (1941–1993). It brings together a selection of Schürmann's as yet unpublished lecture notes, written for the courses he delivered at the New School for Social Research in New York between 1975 and 1993, with previously uncollected essays.

These works offer an additional avenue into the repertoire already available—including recent re-editions of his major philosophical works and of his only novel. The printed works will be complemented by a digital edition of Schürmann's typescripts, along with transcriptions and an extensive critical apparatus.

We hope that the *Selected Writings and Lecture Notes* will contribute to a renewed appreciation of the scope of Schürmann's philosophical endeavor and help to establish him as one of those thinkers who are indispensable for the understanding of our present—or, rather, to show our present as the moment of legibility for Schürmann's work. We are grateful to the Reiner Schürmann Estate for entrusting us with the responsibility of this work and for their full endorsement.